WINE SELF-TALK

15 MINUTES TO RELAX & TAP INTO YOUR INNER GENIUS

KRISTEN HELMSTETTER

Wine Self-Talk

ISBN: 979-8-9850203-4-2

~

This book contains the opinions and ideas of its author. It is intended to provide helpful and informative material on the subjects addressed in the publication; it is not intended to diagnose, prescribe, or treat any health disorder or other serious personal issue, nor is it guaranteeing any particular results. This book is sold with the understanding that the author and publisher are not engaged in rendering medical, health, or any other kind of personal or professional services, and the reader should consult with such person(s) before adopting any of the suggestions in this book or drawing inferences from it. The author and publisher specifically disclaim all responsibility for any liability, loss, or risk, personal or otherwise, which is incurred as a consequence, directly or indirectly, of the use and application of any of the contents of this book.

The author and the publisher of this book will not be held responsible for any misuse of alcohol or any of the information in this book. If you drink alcohol, please do so responsibly and in moderation. Do not drive or operate heavy machinery while under the influence of alcohol.

v1.2

ABOUT THE AUTHOR

In 2018, Kristen Helmstetter sold everything to travel the world with her husband and daughter. She currently lives in a medieval hilltop town in Umbria, Italy.

She writes romance novels under the pen name Brisa Starr.

Listen to *Coffee Self-Talk with Kristen Helmstetter* wherever you listen to podcasts.

You can also find her on Instagram:

instagram.com/coffeeselftalk

OTHER BOOKS BY KRISTEN HELMSTETTER

Coffee Self-Talk: 5 Minutes a Day to Start Living Your Magical Life

The Coffee Self-Talk Daily Readers (#1 & #2): Bite-Sized Nuggets of Magic to Add to Your Morning Routine

Pillow Self-Talk: 5 Minutes Before Bed to Start Living the Life of Your Dreams

The Coffee Self-Talk Guided Journal: Writing Prompts & Inspiration for Living Your Magical Life

The Coffee Self-Talk Blank Journal (blank with lines)

Coffee Self-Talk for Dudes: 5 Minutes a Day to Start Living Your Legendary Life

Coffee Self-Talk for Teen Girls: 5 Minutes a Day for Confidence, Achievement & Lifelong Happiness

COMING SOON

Money Self-Talk (2022)

I dedicate this book to my brother Kenny, a true magician of creativity, a master of both music and engineering.

I love you. Thank you for being an inspiration.

Creativity requires the courage to let go of certainties.

— Erich Fromm

CONTENTS

INTRODUCTION

Dear Friend,

Self-talk changed my life. It took me from feeling lost and unfilled, to doing literal cartwheels from pure joy. Happiness became my new default. Loving life. And soon after that, everything else in my life started going right and falling into place. If you've read my book, *Coffee Self-Talk*, you know the story of how I used a simple, five-minute, morning ritual to transform my life into days that feel glittering and magical... all by changing the words that I say to myself while I sip my morning coffee.

It wasn't long after this daily ritual transformed my life that I started looking for ways to add more self-talk into my day. I craved the high it gave me!

So I started doing a bedtime ritual that I called "Pillow Self-Talk," and I saw equally impressive results there, too. I kept asking myself, *How far can I take this? Where else can I inject more secret sauce for magical living?*

And, although you can let positive affirmations run through your mind all day, there's something special that happens when you attach your self-talk to a specific habit or ritual. Such as your morning coffee, or before bed.

Wine Self-Talk, as an idea, started as a joke in our home. I mean, it sounds awesome, right? It was shortly after I finished writing *Coffee Self-Talk,* and we were living in Italy, where the boxed wine is quite good, and we always had both red and white *on tap*, no corkscrew needed.

Sometime around the dozenth time my husband and I made the joke, I started thinking about the idea seriously.

What if?

What would happen if I linked positive affirmations with the ritual of having a glass of wine?

Wine comes with a few connotations. It's fancy. Drinking a glass is like a special occasion. It's delicious. But most of all, for me anyway, wine is about relaxation. Loosening up. In fact, wine always makes me sleepy, so I never imbibe much, just a few sips, and my husband polishes off whatever is left in my glass.

One evening, I dimmed the lights, poured myself a glass of red, and sat down on my comfy couch with a list of affirmations... my *self-talk script*. I took a sip of the wine, and I started reading the script out loud. Then another sip. Then another.

I'm a lightweight, so it didn't take long, when...

Wow! Amaaaazing! The words in the affirmations felt like they were gliding smoothly from my mouth. That nice, relaxed, swooshy quality (you know, that delicious *wine feeling*) came over me, as it always does. But this time, the feeling was somehow linked to my thoughts, and it seemed to embed itself into the words, and lift them up, giving them special meaning, special importance.

Wine Self-Talk was no joke after all. I was onto something.

My little Wine Self-Talk ritual quickly became an important feature in my life.

First, it was very relaxing. Second, something about the wine made the ritual feel *special*. Imbued with importance, like a ceremony honoring the moment. Even with our boxed wine at the ready, we always had plenty of bottles around—it was Italy, after all, which produces more wine than anybody, even France. I'd often open a bottle for my ritual, to heighten the "special occasion" effect. The graceful, sexy shape of the bottle, the popping-open sound, the rich smell of the cork, the *glug glug* as you pour, the pretty glass... it all enhanced the experience. Self-talk is extra powerful when linked to your senses and emotions. Wine plus self-talk, it turned out, was a *fine pairing*.

I probably could have anticipated both of these effects before my first experiment with Wine Self-Talk. But what happened next was totally unexpected...

Creativity for FREE!

Before I go on, I want to explain what I mean by "creativity." I'm not talking about just your typical "creative" activities, like art, writing, music, etc. Throughout this book, I'm using the word much more broadly, to encompass the wide range of things that can happen when you tap into what I call your *inner genius*.

We all possess this amazing part of our brain that is *freaking incredible*, if we can only manage to tap into it somehow. Your inner genius has the answers. It knows *what to do*. It's able to sift through vast amounts of knowledge hidden away in your memory and your subconscious, look at things sideways, make crazy connections, and come up with ideas that are sometimes so amazing, it feels like they came from someplace outside of you, like a higher intelligence. It feels like *magic*. Like, *Where the hell did that come from? That's brilliant! I did that?*"

This inner genius not only makes creative people creative, it can also make *anybody* smarter about *anything.* Solving business problems. Solving relationship problems. Coming up with better options for yourself. And for your family. Being more clever, funnier, more interesting... the implications are endless. It's about having a superpower that gives you more control over your mind and your actions, and helps you create your magical life.

Ok, back to my wine story...

Readers of *Coffee Self-Talk* will know that I used self-talk to reinvent myself into a novelist, transforming myself from somebody who had literally never written one word of fiction, into a romance author who wrote nine novels in nine months.

As a writer, I pay close attention to my creative process. I need to understand my own abilities, if only to plan my writing schedule. Do I require inspiration? Do I need a whiteboard? Can I write any time of day? Can I write in airports and cafes, or only at my desk? As such, I'm always looking for ways to enhance my creativity. Any little trick not only makes my work easier, it also makes me a better writer.

Wine Self-Talk enhances my creativity "for free." It just happens. Seemingly all by itself. And not just when I'm at my desk writing, but *all the time.* It feels like I've been given some miracle pill from the future, and I'm suddenly capable of thinking in ways that I had never thought before.

Creativity for my writing, creativity for problem-solving in my business, family issues, health... all aspects of life. Anytime I wanted to solve something in my life, I found myself coming at it from new angles, or a different point of view. It was happening every day, and it was fun!

At first, my flashes of insight seemed like a fluke. But it kept on happening. And more often. I even started to expect it. And as my confidence grew—knowing that my inner genius would always be there to help—something wonderful happened... I became *more relaxed than ever.*

I'd been improving my relaxation with my Coffee Self-Talk, but this took it another level. I was experiencing a kind of peace, a notion that *everything is going to be ok. I've got this. I'm equipped to handle whatever comes my way.* Finding solutions to challenges had become easy.

And this gentle confidence settled nicely into what I can only describe as my new, improved, even happier self, because a life with creative zest has more color, more joy, and is a heck of a lot more fun.

In January of 2021, the world started hearing about *Coffee Self-Talk*, and sales went nuts. Readers started joining the book's Facebook group in droves, where it wasn't long before *"How about Wine Self-Talk?"* became a running gag. Someone even posted this cute cartoon:

Which was funny, because I'd been doing my Wine Self-Talk ritual, but I'd never talked about it. Great minds think alike, right?

By then, I had come to understand the benefits of connecting self-talk with wine in this super nice, relaxing ritual. So I decided to write a book about it, and here it is.

I don't recommend drinking alcohol too frequently or in large amounts. That's your call, and you know what's best for you. This ritual, although designed with a bit of alcohol in mind, doesn't require it. Personally, I don't drink very much (just two or three sips), but I recognize the power of combining alcohol with a deeply profound ritual, and there is a body of scientific literature associating cognitive enhancement with modest consumption of alcohol.

You can approach this relaxing ritual on a nightly basis, with or without alcohol. Or you can choose to do it only once or twice a week, depending on your goals. For me, Wine Self-Talk is a weekly ritual where I take stock of my goals for the week, and I plant "creative seeds" that take root and flower in the following days and weeks.

If you don't drink alcohol, no problem. Feel free to have sparkling water with a wedge of lemon or orange, in a beautiful wine glass. Or kombucha. Or select a special beverage that you only drink during this ritual.

It is my heart-felt intention that this book helps you tap into your innate wellspring of knowledge, unleashing your dazzling brilliance, your *inner genius*. Whatever immediate application you might have in mind, I'd encourage you to think broader... there are virtually no limits to what you can accomplish once you've harnessed the cognitive superpower of your creative essence and acquired the confidence to go boldly forward and attempt big things.

Like, *really big* things. The stuff that magical lives are made of.

Have fun with this!

All my very best,

Kristen

P.S. Shoot me an email to share your experiences doing Wine Self-Talk, and to receive a free PDF with goodies, including a *bonus chapter* and *starter questions* for your Wine Self-Talk ritual.

Email me at:

Kristen@KristenHelmstetter.com

Please specify that you'd like the "*Wine Self-Talk goodies.*"

HOW TO USE THIS BOOK

This book is divided into two parts.

In Part I, you'll discover what self-talk is, and why it's so powerful. I'll also explain why creativity is so important for living a magical life, whether you think of yourself as a creative person or not. It's worth stating right now: We all have the potential to be *wildly creative*, and this book will help you tap into this fundamental human capability. Every one of us possesses an inner genius, just waiting to be unleashed. And lastly, I'll teach you an incredible brain hack, *Wine Self-Talk*—a relaxing, fifteen-minute ritual for unleashing this inner genius.

In Part II, I've provided 16 lessons, each with a specially designed Wine Self-Talk script to accompany the lesson. You will use these scripts, or scripts you write yourself, when you do your Wine Self-Talk ritual.

Each of these lessons deals with some aspect of creativity. You can use the provided scripts as is, or feel free to make changes to them, as affirmations are more powerful when they use words that resonate strongly with you.

When you've completed Part I, you'll be ready to begin doing your Wine Self-Talk ritual. You might choose to go through one lesson per week, perhaps setting aside a regular special time, such as Friday nights. Or you might prefer to first read through all of Part II, and then go back to the lessons that seem most relevant to your current situation.

A BRIEF WORD ABOUT WINE

Note: Wine is not required to do the activities in this book.

~

This book describes a fun, relaxing ritual involving the optional consumption of wine. If you have any issues with drinking alcohol, or if you simply prefer not to, you may substitute any non-alcoholic beverage and still get benefits from this book and from positive self-talk.

If you choose to drink an alcoholic beverage while doing this, please do so responsibly and in moderation. If you're slurring, drooling, passing out on the pavement, or texting old lovers, you've gone too far.

PART I

TAPPING INTO YOUR INNER GENIUS

CHAPTER 1

SELF-TALK FOR LIVING YOUR MAGICAL LIFE

Chance favors the prepared mind.

— Louis Pasteur

Somewhere deep inside of you lies all the answers you seek. Answers to questions. Solutions to make your problems go away. Ways to make your stress and anxiety vaporize. Ways to make your dreams come true. Ways to live your magical life.

In this book, I'm going to teach you a relaxing, 15-minute ritual that combines positive self-talk with wine (or whatever beverage you prefer) to tap into this source of brilliance, your inner genius.

Positive Self-Talk for the Most Amazing Life

The day I made self-talk part of my daily strategy was the day my life changed. Using self-talk, a technique so simple that a five-year-old can do it, I transformed from living as a stressed-out, hot mess with no real direction or sense of purpose, to living a life of glittering sunshine, happiness, peace, and fulfillment.

This transformation was complete, from head to toe. And best of all, it was *fast*.

What is self-talk?

Self-talk is simply the words you think and say about yourself and your life. It's the dialog that runs in your head all day long. It's the thoughts that fill the hours of your day. It's your outlook on life. Your beliefs. It's what is playing in your mind when you watch the news, or go on a walk, or as you fall asleep at night.

As you can imagine, there are many varieties of words and thoughts in your brain. Some words are happy and loving; others are crappy and sad. There are uplifting, empowering thoughts, and there are debilitating and depressing thoughts.

These words and thoughts matter. They are, in fact, the primary factor that determines what kind of life you'll have. How happy you'll be. The reason they are so important is that they, more than anything else, determine your actions. Your *behavior*. Whether or not you make good decisions or bad, take risks or hold yourself back, invest in yourself or squander your time, and how well you handle the bumps on the road of life... these are all determined by your self-talk.

When you speak or think thoughts, you are actually giving instructions to your brain. And your brain will do whatever you tell it. If you say, "I'm always so tired," well, guess what? You just told your brain to make sure that you'll be tired. Tell it you never have enough money, and that'll be true, too. On the other hand, if you tell your brain you have boundless energy, or that you're a money magnet, then your brain will act on these instructions instead.

Your brain doesn't care if what you tell it is true or false. It will act on the instructions either way. It doesn't care whether you choose positive or negative words. This gives you incredible power. The words you use are *your choice*. No matter what. It's always *you* who is choosing which instructions you give to your brain.

Your brain not only directs your actions, it also directs your focus. It filters what you pay attention to, and what you ignore. It makes you see things in your world that support that focus. In this way, it affects your version of *reality*.

For instance, if you wake up every day and think you're fat, or unattractive, or boring, or unworthy, then your brain thinks that that's what you want it to focus on, and that's exactly what it does.

On the other hand, if you wake up in the morning feeling jazzed and optimistic about all the opportunities in your life, confident that success is in the palm of your hand, feeling and thinking you're beautiful, and when you come from a foundation of self-love and worthiness, then you can bet your ass that your brain is going to make damn sure you see more of *that* in your life. It's going to shine a bright spotlight on the things that support that uplifting thought pattern.

It really is this simple...

You have a brain, and *it wants you to tell it what to do!*

When you start to speak and think positively about yourself, your life, and the world, you soon just naturally start to feel more positive. And as you feel more positive, you say more positive things, in a virtuous cycle. This combination of positive thinking and feeling is what accelerates you in a rocket ship to your destiny and dreams.

So, that is self-talk. The words you say, and the thoughts you think. When you "do" positive self-talk, it simply means you're taking conscious control of the process, retraining how your brain speaks by using positive affirmations, which replace negative thoughts and words with positive ones. This can happen through a formal process using self-talk scripts such as those provided in Part II, or it can be throughout the day, as you go about your life. Ideally, it's both.

The Emotional Connection

But there's another element I haven't mentioned yet. An element that makes the retraining process happen much faster. And that is, to link your positive self-talk with *positive emotions*.

The way to use self-talk for rapid, *lightning-fast* change in your life, is to combine those positive words and thoughts in your brain *with positive feelings in your heart*. You might imagine that, when you think good things, you'd naturally feel good things. But that's not always the case, especially when people first start, and especially if they're dealing with a lifetime of bad self-talk to overcome.

When you come from a place of real negativity—darkness, or depression, or anxiety—it's easy to feel like positive words won't help, like they don't hold much power. So, while you might *say* things that are positive, you might still *feel* doubtful. The good news is, even if this is the case, even if you don't feel it yet, you will in time. Especially if you repeat your self-talk scripts regularly, over and over, drilling the new way of speaking into your brain through sheer repetition. The more you do it, the more your brain fires and wires these thoughts into the neuronal pathways in your brain, making them permanent.

And as this happens, you do start to believe it more, and the more you believe it, *the more you feel it*. These feelings change your energy, and that's a good thing. You want those good vibes! They make it start to feel real. So, anything you can do to reinforce these emotions helps get the ball rolling, including pretending, like you're a method actor, in which you "get into character" as your new, improved self. This will help speed up the process. Basically, *fake it till you make it*.

So there you go, thinking happy and feeling happy—the ultimate combination for manifesting your magical life.

The Power of Self-Love

Another incredible benefit of positive self-talk is that it improves your self-love and your self-esteem, which changes the way you show up to the world every day. It changes the way you get out of bed. It changes the way you walk. It changes the way you sit at your desk. It changes how you speak to people. It changes everything about your behavior when it comes to confidence and courage. You become more curious, and this automatically sets your mind up for success. Self-esteem creates the playing field for ideas to zigzag around in your brain, crash into each other, and create new things. Because you're not afraid, and because you feel, *deep-down*, that you are truly worthy of the good that may come from your explorations.

This makes you feel really good. Beaming with confidence. And it turns out, this feeling of confidence isn't hocus-pocus. It's not make-believe. Your self-talk actually affects the secretion of chemicals in your brain—neurotransmitters known as "feel good" chemicals... dopamine, serotonin, and endorphins—that make you, well, *feel good*, and more likely to succeed.

As I described in *Coffee Self-Talk*, when we were living in a small apartment in northern Italy, I started doing self-talk each morning with my coffee. I had no grand expectations... no expectations at all, really. I just knew that I liked how it made me feel, right then, in the moment, as I was doing it. Soon, that nice, happy feeling swelled to fill my entire day. Something was happening to me. Something great! After two weeks, these happy feelings were still showing no signs of slowing down, and I finally told my husband what I had been doing. I kept doing my Coffee Self-Talk ritual, every morning without fail, for months. And things just kept getting better and better. My self-talk planted little golden seeds in my mind that grew and blossomed, manifesting into pure butterfly transformation. I'm talking *Phoenix-from-ashes* stuff. No anxiety, feeling relaxed, happy, and at peace. Totally epic living.

I started manifesting the best life, which included making more money (in unexpected ways), waking up happy and zesty, feeling curious for the upcoming day, stronger love with my husband, more quality time with my daughter, and a heart, soul, and pace of life that came from a state of flowing and ease.

I could go on and on, which I sort of did in *Coffee Self-Talk*. In that book, I spend a lot of time going into much detail about how and why self-talk can help you live the most amazing life, what I call a *magical* life. How it can help make your dreams come true. How it can blast you into the happiness stratosphere. And how it can really make all the difference. And, of course, how to actually do the morning ritual.

Whenever an interviewer asks me how to improve life, or reduce stress, or how to smash through goals, or love yourself more, or how to be happier... *my answer is always the same*. It comes down to your self-talk.

How can this one thing, self-talk, be so powerful?

As I described above, it's because self-talk changes the way you think about yourself. Your positive self-talk changes the way you think about the world. It changes how you *interact* with the world. It changes what you attract into your life. It changes what you focus on. It changes everything... in particular, what you believe is possible.

But above all, it changes how you feel about yourself. It makes it possible to *truly love yourself*. No matter what you've been through. No matter what you believe about yourself, right or wrong. And the reason self-love is so important is because, if you don't love yourself, it doesn't matter how hard you work, or what strategies you attempt —whether for losing weight, or making money, or accomplishing anything hard—if you don't love yourself, you won't feel worthy of succeeding, and your subconscious will sabotage you. It'll wreck your otherwise perfectly good plans.

For this reason, I always include lines to reinforce self-love in all of my scripts, including those in Part II.

CHAPTER 2

YOUR INNER GENIUS

There is no doubt that creativity is the most important human resource of all. Without creativity, there would be no progress, and we would be forever repeating the same patterns.

— EDWARD DE BONO

Did you know that butterflies have super cool vision? Humans have three color receptors, which combine to allow us to see all the colors we see in the rainbow. But there are way more colors in light than we can see. Butterflies have four receptors, which allows them to see more colors than we do.

But that's nothing... the Australian Swallowtail butterfly puts them all to shame, with *fifteen* different receptors. Each of which can see its own range of the spectrum, including ultraviolet light!

Can you imagine what it would be like to see the world through the eyes of an Australian Swallowtail butterfly for just a few seconds? It would be *mind-blowing!*

Our picture of reality is limited by our perception. There are things that exist that we simply can't see. There are sound frequencies that we can't hear. There are magnetic fields that some animals can sense, but we're oblivious to. And bats can "see" in total darkness using sound. What would that even "look" like? I can't even imagine *hearing* the shape of, say, a car or a spoon.

Here's a little test: Close your eyes, and try to imagine a color you've never seen before.

You can't!

Similarly, our thoughts are limited by what we know. And what we believe is possible.

For all of recorded history, nobody had ever run a mile in less than four minutes. Nobody believed it was humanly possible. That is, until Roger Bannister did it on May 6, 1954, clocking in at 3 minutes, 59.4 seconds.

And then, 46 days later, somebody else did it even faster.

It had been possible *all along*. It's just that nobody *believed it*.

Nobody thought to make a phone with a touchscreen interface. Then Steve Jobs and the engineers at Apple did it. Within weeks, competitors were announcing their plans to develop their own touchscreen phones.

Nobody thought it was possible to launch things into space using reusable rockets. That is, until Elon Musk and SpaceX proved it could be done *in style*, by having the rockets fly themselves back to the launch pad and *land upright*, ready to be reused! And in the process, reducing the cost of space flight to a fraction of its former cost. As of this writing, China, France, and at least eight aerospace companies are all developing their own reusable rockets. One of their CEOs even went so far as to say that any rocket company that wasn't working on reusable rockets would go out of business.

Why is it so difficult to imagine things we've never witnessed?

It actually has a name: *failure of imagination*.

Failure of imagination applies to ordinary people's lives as well. Prior to it becoming widespread, many people never even imagined working from home, for instance. Neither did their employers. With COVID, it became normal for many kinds of jobs.

When I told people that we were going to sell everything and travel the world for a few years, working from our laptops, so many people told us they'd love to do that, but they could never afford it. But guess what? We slashed our expenses *dramatically* when we left the country! No more rent/mortgage, no car payment, no cable bill, no crazy U.S. healthcare insurance, etc. We traveled all over Europe, living mostly rent-free, by housesitting. That is, taking care of people's homes and pets while the owners are away on vacation. Or by staying in charming but dirt-cheap places, like Bansko, a ski resort town in Bulgaria, where you can rent a modern, furnished apartment for $250 a month, and a family of three can eat a delicious dinner out for about $20.

Most people we run into never even knew these options existed. Even among fellow long-term travelers!

It begs the question... *What other options—for anything—exist, that we don't know about?*

~

What if there were a way to see what others can't see?

What if there were a way to imagine possibilities that do exist, but you haven't imagined them yet?

What if there were a way to create what others haven't created?

What if there were solutions to the problems in your life, but you just didn't know they existed? What if there were a way to find them?

There is a way to do all of these: *Wine Self-Talk.*

And it works by tapping into your *inner genius.*

~

Say Hello to Your Inner Genius

I mentioned earlier that we all have an *inner genius* that's capable of amazing mental and creative feats. It's part of our subconscious, and it's similar to our intuition, in that it's powerful, brilliant, and we all have one, but most people aren't really in tune with it.

But the inner genius I'm referring to is not the same as your intuition. Your intuition is like a black-box computer, making calculations behind the scenes, and spitting out answers that come to you in the form of hunches. Or emotions, like fear.

Whereas the inner genius I'm talking about is your *creative source.* It's where all of your *aha* moments come from. Epiphanies. Flashes of insight. Eureka moments.

And of course, it's the inspiration that goes into all of the things we think of as "creative," such as drawing, painting, sculpting, writing, singing, dancing, and playing music. And far more activities that perhaps don't leap to mind, but they are indeed creative: cooking, knitting, sewing, crafting, making YouTube videos, inventing, engineering, starting businesses, launching products, and building Web sites.

Creativity even applies to coming up with new ideas in fields that most people don't think of as creative at all: math (inventing new proofs), finance (inventing new financial instruments), management (solving problems in new ways), and even accounting... although one CPA I knew was a little *too* creative—*lol...* he's now wearing an orange jumpsuit at Club Fed!

And perhaps the most overlooked category of creativity of all: those daily little ingenuities that solve micro-problems and remove friction from our lives. Like clever household repairs involving whatever materials you have on hand. Or whatever genius invented the idea of using a bear clip (it's like a large paperclip) attached to the edge of a desk, on which you can hang your phone's charging cable, so that you don't have to reach down to the floor every time your phone needs some juice.

These little innovations add up! In fact, half of living a magical life is just removing the tiny irritants in life, polishing it to a shimmery shine!

Creativity also comes in the form of generating new ideas. Any new idea, in fact. It could be thinking of what to make for dinner. Or thinking of a different way to explain something to your child, when the old explanation wasn't working. Or thinking of a new activity or vacation destination. Did you know there's a hotel in Finland where you can sleep in warm, cozy, glass igloos and look up at the Northern Lights as you drift off to sleep? There are also Viking summer camps where kids live in recreated Viking villages and learn to make Viking stuff. Where was this when I was a kid?

So, creativity comes in all forms. But every form involves either creating something or doing something in a new way. And these are exactly what your inner genius does.

Your inner genius does these things by sidestepping your normal thought processes. You see, our normal mode of thinking is mostly concerned with efficiency. Doing the same things, the same ways, using as little effort as possible. And this is a great way for a brain to work.

Except when it isn't.

When we're faced with novel challenges, we need novel solutions. And even when we're doing stuff we've been doing for ages, sometimes it's just time to take a new look, and see if there's a better way.

Maybe technology has changed. Or social norms. Or some other thing that makes the old solution outdated.

And sometimes, it's just time for a change. Change for the sake of change.

These are all times when your inner genius is better suited to the task than your normal-mode brain.

Unfortunately, as I've mentioned, most people are not in touch with their inner genius. Why is this? All kids are very creative. It's an innate human ability. Most people somehow lose it. Some people say our educational system discourages creative thinking. Or maybe it's just a variant of the old saying, you can't teach an old dog new tricks. Like, maybe we just stop generating new solutions for something once we've found a solution that's "good enough." And eventually, we've got good-enough solutions to most common problems. And then, from using it less, the creativity skill atrophies like an unused muscle.

Who knows. But it doesn't matter. You've got this muscle, and if you exercise it, it will grow and get stronger. No matter how uncreative you think you are, I promise, that can change. And if you already think of yourself as creative, that's great! The techniques in this book will help you take it to the next level.

~

Wine Self-Talk was designed to increase your creativity, and it might surprise you at how profound this is *for living your most magical life*. By the end of this book, you'll be inspired to make creativity a permanent part of your life because of how amazing it makes you *feel*. How it helps you manifest your dreams and goals faster. How much happier your days are.

It's true. Living a creative life is like taking a daily *happy-joy* pill. The funny thing to me is that I had *no idea* this would be the case. I never knew creativity played such a vital role with *happiness*. But when my creativity flourished, because of training my brain for it, I started to feel different. Inside. Like a spark had ignited in my soul, and then it grew, and now, the fire is blazing in all the colors that those crazy Australian butterflies can see! It makes me feel phenomenal! And wow, my life is so much more interesting now.

And, just to repeat: *Anyone can do it.*

> *The key question isn't 'What fosters creativity?' But it is why in god's name isn't everyone creative? Where was the human potential lost? How was it crippled? I think therefore a good question might be not why do people create? But why do people not create?*
>
> — Abraham Maslow

Creativity for Living Your Most Magical Life

Here's the plain truth: Life sucks without creativity. There. I said it. It's boring. Creativity brings so many cool benefits. In particular, it's a powerful force for helping you live a sparkly, magical life. How? Because it feels *amazing* to be creative. To think creatively. To actually *make stuff*. It's a huge self-esteem booster, and your confidence soars when you start finding creative solutions to all sorts of problems, or when you start coming up with great ideas. And then, your stress levels decrease!

How?

Well, success begets success. When you start living every day from a foundation of creativity, whenever a challenge pops up, or if you need a new idea for something, you'll have this amazing confidence in your ability to deal with it. It becomes your new *normal*. You come to expect that your creativity *will come*, because you have strengthened your creativity muscle. Problems aren't a big deal anymore, because you know you'll figure something out. Imagine a life like that, having total trust and confidence in your own abilities. And the more often you do this, the easier it becomes. Wine Self-Talk helps you get there in two big ways: the *Minus* and the *Plus*.

The "Minus" refers to things you don't like that creativity can help solve. Problems, challenges, hurdles, obstacles, etc. They exist, and they're part of life, no biggie. In fact, solving them starts to become its own reward, once you get good at it. Once you have faith in your ability as a problem-solver.

Have you seen the movie, *The Martian*? If you haven't, stream it *tonight*. If you've already seen it, watch it again! Even if you're not into sci-fi, that doesn't matter. Matt Damon plays an astronaut who gets stranded alone on Mars, and he has to figure out how to survive. It's an amazing story, because he has one insane problem after another thrown at him, and he freakin' figures something out, one after another, using his brilliant what?... *Creativity!* It's so inspiring, watching him solve ridiculously hard problems that would make most of us curl up into little balls of sniveling astronaut.

You might say, "Well Kristen, that's all fine and good, but Damon plays an astronaut with all these science and engineering skills... that's not me." Well that's fine, you know why? Because you're also not stranded on freaking Mars. You've got all these resources at your disposal: YouTube, Amazon, Home Depot, the public library... even our own cozy, supportive Facebook group! (Facebook.com/groups/cof-feeselftalk) Whatever your situation is, there is a solution, and you *can figure it out!* There's always a way.

And then, there's the *Plus*.

The "Plus" refers to the *positive* uses for creativity in your life. The wonderful things you seek in life. The aspirational things. Your goals. In fact, if you can't name your goals or your aspirations, right now, without thinking about it, then you need to get on that shit and write some down, because people who set goals famously do two things that other people don't do: 1) They *achieve* a heckuva lot of those goals, and 2) they actually *live longer*. Yes, it's true, people who set goals and identify as having a purpose in life have higher life expectancy.

And this plus side is where the beauty of creativity really shines. It's not just solving problems, it's creating new things, making art, expressing yourself, and seeing the world in amazing, new ways. It's thinking outside the box, making new connections—*all the time*—and generally being more adaptable in your thinking, and curious about the world.

Wine Self-Talk is designed specifically to address both the minus and the plus. That is, to help you solve problems, as well as help you blossom into the beautiful, self-actualized spirit that you were meant to be.

CHAPTER 3

SIX GIFTS FROM CREATIVITY

> Creativity is the power to connect the seemingly unconnected.
>
> — William Plomer

I've outlined some of the benefits of creativity in the previous chapter, but for our purposes with your relaxing Wine Self-Talk ritual, we can think of the benefits in six categories:

1. Magical Living
2. Creating Options for Yourself
3. Problem Squashing
4. Long-Term Relaxation
5. Epic Ideas & Imagination
6. Sparkling Health & Wellbeing

Let's take a moment and look at each of these, so that you'll grasp the full magnitude of how important this is, and get you pumped about starting the ritual.

1. Magical Living

When I think of the word "creative" or "creativity," I automatically envision sparkles and magic. Curlicues, curiosity, and questions. Perhaps it's because, when I used to think of creativity, I always pictured images of fantasy and pure imagination. Yellow brick road stuff, wizards. Colors. Music. Artists wearing long, denim skirts in Taos, New Mexico, painting epic Southwestern landscapes with bold strokes of dazzling colors. And with pictures like these in mind, it just makes sense that, when you have more creativity in your life, you'd automatically live a more magical experience!

But there's more to creativity than that. And there's more than just the results you get from living creatively and being a creative being. That is, the act of creating itself is intrinsically satisfying. Deeply. And this is how creativity, no matter what form it takes, no matter what you actually do with it, makes you legit happier, which *does* make a more magical life.

In my book, *Coffee Self-Talk*, I drive home the importance of thinking and feeling elevated thoughts and emotions for legendary living. In other words, think nice thoughts and feel nice feelings... to live a magical life. By folding creativity into the mix, we're taking things to the *next level.*

What is a magical life?

Magical living is a life in which you're very happy most of the time! You're in a great mood. Anxiety and stress, big or small, are *dramatically* decreased. Sometimes even to zero. If you do have a downer day, it's minor and minimal, a tiny blemish. Here, healed, and then gone.

A magical life is full of jaw-dropping synchronicities, events in your life lining up, almost, well... magically. It's setting goals and smashing through them with glittery energy bombs, and attracting and manifesting amazing things, whether that's health, or wealth, or love. That's magical living. And it's incredible.

It's waking up every day feeling curious and excited. Feeling purpose and drive, which fuel every step you take toward realizing your dream life. You feel encouraged to express yourself, as the best, most beautiful, authentic version of you. And creativity plays a *huge* part of this.

For most of my life, I didn't consider myself as creative, even after writing many nonfiction books. I mean, *come on*, nonfiction as creative? I always figured I was just conveying facts, or repackaging research I had done. You know, a kind of technical skill, but not "creative." But it was my husband who pointed out one day that, in my own kitchen, I had developed over 500 recipes for these books, and there's literally no better word for that than *creative*.

Huh, I realized. *I guess that's right.* The problem had been that I was using too narrow a definition of the word. And as a result, I didn't identify with it. Which had made me think that, while there are creative people out there... I just wasn't one of them.

Well, that's not only a crappy mindset, it's just plain wrong. I laugh at my old self now. I know better. Because, absolutely, nonfiction is just as creative as cooking is, and gardening is, and so is picking out a great outfit, dancing, ventriloquism, journaling, or for that matter, telling stories, or embellishing gossip with wild gestures and exaggerated expressions, and making your friends laugh hysterically. (*Hi, Mom!*)

If you really want to drill down into the science of why living a creative life makes for magical living, here's the short answer: Because using that part of your brain puts you in *flow state* more often. "Flow" is a mental state that psychologists have studied in all kinds of situations. It's this incredible state of mind where time flies, and whatever you're working on feels seamless and exciting. You're immersed in it. Effortless. You're *in the zone*. You're at one with what you're doing, whether that's making something beautiful, practicing a skill, or inventing a new product. When my husband is tinkering in the garage, or making something out of wood or metal, or designing something in Photoshop, he will literally go hours and hours, not even realizing that he hasn't eaten yet that day. You get into this kind of mode that's fun and stimulating, yet also strangely relaxing, which makes it easy to just go, and go, and go.

In a way, it's like a mild *state of bliss*.

The state of flow feels wonderful, and it occurs when your brain is enjoying either alpha brain waves or theta brain waves (theta waves happen when you're drifting off to sleep). Both of which feel fabulous, are relaxing, and are part of the creative process. When I'm in flow, I'm massively more productive. When I'm in flow, any and all fears vanish, my learning accelerates, and my creativity sparkles like diamonds in my mind.

So, yeah, being in flow feels incredible, and it feels like magical living. But unlike many peak states, the flow you get into when creating is easy to attain and highly replicable. You can literally do it every day, time permitting. It can become your habit. Your routine. And with this elevated feeling saturating your soul on a daily basis, you can see how easy it would be to attract and draw your dreams closer to you, because your average energy level is such a high vibe.

But here's the other thing about magical living from adding more creativity to your life. Your confidence goes *through the roof*. At first, if you're new to making creativity a part of your life—or more precisely, if you don't *identify* as a creative person—then you naturally might approach it more shyly. But that's where Wine Self-Talk comes in. It's super helpful for leveling up your *boldness*. And once you get into the habit and start to identify in this new way, the creative mindset becomes more natural to you, creative thinking becomes second nature, your intuition improves, your skills increase through practice, and your confidence about using creativity as a tool in your magical-living toolkit blooms.

As I mentioned earlier, living your best life comes from a foundation of self-love and worthiness. Positive self-talk, like the kind you'll find in the scripts in Part II, helps you build a powerful foundation of worthiness and that automatically boosts your confidence. Good news, this starts to happen right away, even before you start injecting more creative thinking into your life.

And last, but not least, creativity makes a *fun life*. I mean, think of it this way... what were some of your favorite things to do as a kid? It's likely that art was high on the list. Or puzzles and games (problem-solving). Or playing dolls (storytelling). All of that is creativity. As you start to do the grown-up version of these things that your brain was designed to do, your life just naturally gets more *fun*.

2. Creating Options for Yourself

> *The best way to predict the future is to create it.*
>
> — Peter Drucker

Power is the ability to act. To do what you want. Do you want to be free to make your own decisions? To pursue your dreams? To live your magical life?

These all require having power. Again, *the ability to act. To do what you want.*

But where does power come from?

Power comes from *having options*.

Don't like your job? The person with a dozen job offers from other companies has *options*. The person with a million dollars in the bank has *options*. They have leverage in negotiations.

When you run out of options, you lose your power. For this reason, one of the greatest benefits of tapping into your inner genius is to ask it to *generate options* for you. And your inner genius is very good at answering questions that you pose to it.

You: *Hello, Inner Genius. Here's my situation... What are my options?*

Inner Genius: *Good question. Let me get to work on that. Got any wine?*

Haha.

Have you seen *Limitless*, the 2011 movie starring Bradley Cooper?

The film is a sci-fi thriller, with a fascinating premise: A guy (Bradley) is stuck in a rut in life. He's going nowhere, having worked on writing a book since... forever, but making no progress, can't pay his rent, lives in squalor, and so on. One day, somebody gives him this pill, an experimental smart drug. Moments later, Bradley's brain becomes insanely perceptive, noticing every tiny detail around him. He suddenly has instant access to every neuron in his brain, every bit of information he's encountered in his life, including everything he never noticed, or forgot, and it gives him, like, a million IQ. Superhero-level stuff. And from there, things get wild.

Bradley gets into trouble with bad guys, and he uses his smart pills to get himself out of impossible situations, such as instantly knowing martial arts, because he once saw experts fight on TV when he was a kid.

Talk about accessing your inner genius!

Will Wine Self-Talk do this for you?

I wish!

No, but there's a useful parallel. The movie presents an irresistible question... What if we could access all of our brain? What could we do with that?

What *options* could we see, that we can't see now?

What options could we *create*, that don't exist now?

Imagine having the mental faculties to *think your way* out of any situation. You would be, well, *limitless*.

And... you sort of *do* have such mental faculties. In theory, anyway. You kind of are *limitless*.

I mean, sure, some problems are beyond human control. Some problems might actually have no solution. But for everything else, the limitations are largely based on our inability to *know what to do*.

Options. What if your brain was really good at coming up with options?

You would be able to do almost anything.

There are lots of techniques, exercises, books, and classes about developing your creativity. We're really just scratching the surface here, and I encourage you to explore them if this is something that interests you. But I have never found a simpler, easier, more fun path toward developing creativity—tapping into your *inner genius*—than Wine Self-Talk.

Any technique you come across that teaches you new ways to expand your creativity, or come up with new options on the fly, is worth checking out. But so far as I know, none of them involve drinking delicious, relaxing wine!

3. Problem-Squashing

Creative thinking helps you with any problems in your life. It can help you solve financial problems. It can help you solve health problems. It can help you solve relationship problems. So, amping up your creativity skills is going to help you with every single thing in your life. Sometimes by helping you figure out immediate solutions. Other times, it helps you figure out a roadmap toward a long-term solution, where you'll figure out the details later. Sometimes it will help you solve problems by generating new options, as described above. And finally, sometimes it will help you avoid problems in the first place!

How does creativity help you do all of these things? Thinking creatively essentially makes you *smarter...* by making more, and new, connections in your brain that were previously not happening. It's that simple. Ideas come together in new and novel ways, and you have more eureka moments. As Steve Jobs said,

Creativity is just connecting things.

Start making connections, and you release your inner genius! Once you do that, you'll step into your life and lean into problems, big and small, with more swagger. More confidence. More brainpower. Once you've developed this capability, you won't mind when a challenge comes your way because you'll just grab your baseball bat and knock it out of the park.

4. Long-Term Relaxation

Wine Self-Talk is relaxing the moment you do it. That's short-term relaxation, and it's wonderful.

But what we all really want, is long-term relaxation. Relief from stress and anxiety. Wine Self-Talk can help with that, too. To explain, it's worth taking a moment to look at the interesting, chicken-and-egg relationship between relaxation and creativity.

When you're in a creative state, or a *flow state*, your anxiety and stress are reduced. Stress limits blood flow in your brain, which forces your resource-starved brain to stay hyper-focused, which prevents it from making connections across different places in your mind. Those precious creativity connections go dark. No glitter. No illumination. No genius flashes of insight.

Mark Beeman, Professor of Psychology at Northwestern University, says,

The more anxiety we experience, the fewer insights we have.

If you're under a lot of stress, or crushed with anxiety, the solutions that you need can only be seen... when you *aren't feeling stressed or anxious!*

What the hell? That's not fair. It's a mental trap!

Stress can freeze you solid, like ice. This makes it darn near impossible to come up with new ideas at the time you need them most. The answers might be down there, somewhere, deep in your subconscious... but you have no way to access them when you're stressed out.

It's funny to me now, but not long ago, I never dreamed that having a *creativity mindset* could be the key to solving life's most stressful problems, like financial problems, or problems at work, or any problems for that matter. That's because I didn't understand what creativity is really about. I thought creativity was fashion design. Poetry. Songwriting. It was *not* how you get out of debt, or embark on a new career, or break through to a troubled teenager. I was closed-minded, with a cement wall around my narrow conception of what the word meant.

Creativity is an incredible tool—*for everything in life*. Yes, painting and stuff... but also for so much more. Creativity is basically a kind of *intelligence*. It even has all these great synonyms: *inspiration, inventiveness, ingenuity, originality, resourcefulness, enterprise, innovation.*

When this realization hit me, a wrecking ball blasted through that cement wall. My life would never be the same. I quickly saw that creativity was fundamental to living a magical life. Maybe even *required*.

I'm sure you can think of a time when you were so stressed that you felt closed-in, tightness in your chest. I've been there, and it sucks! You want to curl up in the fetal position. In such a state, you are not expansive or open-minded enough to hear the helpful whispers from the universe or your inner genius.

When you're stressed, the brain changes its blood flow to support intense focus. But when the answers aren't coming to you, that sometimes results in becoming stuck in an obsessive, unrelenting loop. This blocks all creativity, by preventing your brain from taking a step back and casting a wider view, and looking for less conventional solutions.

When you're stressed and over-analyzing everything, your brain can get stuck in a state of beta brain waves, which give you a heightened state of alertness and critical reasoning. Beta brain waves are great when you need them, such as many mental tasks at your job, paying bills, following a recipe, and so on. But it can get out of control and result in too much anxiety, arousal, adrenaline, and an inability to relax.

At times like this, you need a way to make your beta brain waves settle down and make room for alpha brain waves—those are the flowy, feel-good waves. When you're surfing alpha brain waves, you're more day-dreamy, open-minded, and relaxed. You see things from different perspectives, make new connections, and come up with new ideas.

Anxiety and tension represent a full-frontal assault to your creativity. It freezes it, like ice. No flow mode, and you get stuck in what I call the *Cycle of Stress*:

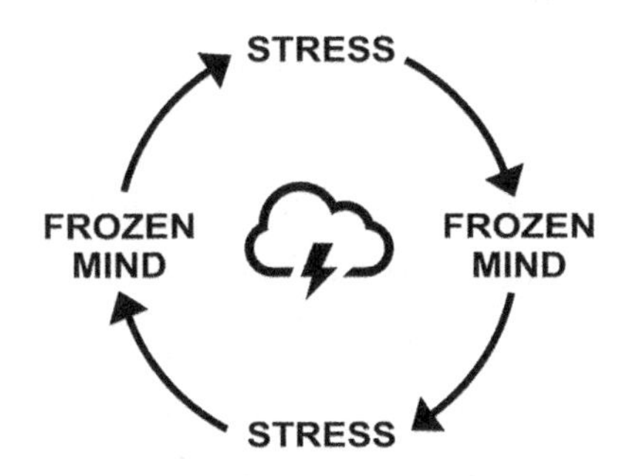

So, how do you break out of this debilitating Cycle of Stress?

There is another cycle, the opposite of the Cycle of Stress, which I call the *Cycle of Solutions*. It looks like this:

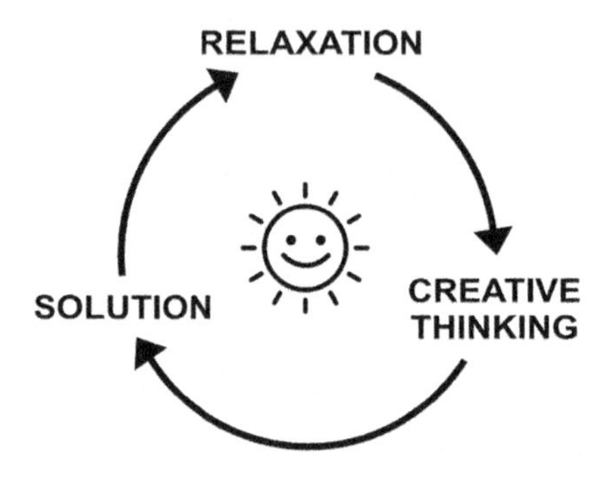

Imagine you're faced with a problem. In the Cycle of Solutions, if you start out in a good frame of mind (not stressed, you're relaxed, alpha brain waves), you're *much* more likely to come up with a solution to your problem. And then, when the problem is solved, it makes you relax. When you're relaxed, you're better at thinking creatively, and so the cycle repeats.

In this way, you are able to solve complex problems by breaking them down into mini-problems, and working your way through each of them, one by one, using the power of your creative mind to craft a series of mini-solutions to each mini-problem.

Notice I said, "If you start out in a good frame of mind..."

That's the key.

If you start out stressed, the Cycle of Solutions never spins up. It never gets going. Instead, you can easily find yourself stuck in the Cycle of Stress.

If you start out relaxed, you're good to go. But what do you do when you're stuck in Stressville without a bus ticket?

Wine Self-Talk to the rescue!

Wine Self-Talk is your bus ticket out of Stressville.

One of the wonderful features of self-talk is that you can do it... *even when you're hair-on-fire stressed.* You don't need to wait until you're happy, or "in the mood," or "feeling it." You can do self-talk even when you feel like everything is falling apart. And best of all, *it still works.*

Wine Self-Talk operates on your stressed-out brain as what's called a *pattern interrupt.* There are other pattern interrupts, a famous example being in old movies when somebody is freaking out, and somebody else slaps them, or splashes cold water on their face, immediately bringing the person back to his senses.

With Wine Self-Talk, when you do the ritual, the combination of the relaxing wine, the relaxed vibe of the set-and-setting (dim lights, quiet, etc.), and the carefully chosen words of your self-talk script... these combine powerfully to *break the pattern* of your beta brain waves, ushering in a relaxed, calm state of alpha wave flow.

In times of extreme stress, you can repeat your script, over and over, for even an hour, sipping your wine, and somewhat mesmerizing yourself into a mildly hypnotic trance. This is not new... practitioners of meditation and self-hypnosis have been doing something similar for ages. I don't generally identify Wine Self-Talk with these, only because this is just the extreme case. In most situations, such intensity is not necessary, and the normal, 10 or 15-minute Wine Self-Talk ritual is plenty.

That said, even when there is no big crisis, you might want to experiment with this extended format, to delve even deeper into your *creative source*, just to see what happens. For best results, be sure to avoid drinking too much, by slowing down the pace of your wine consumption.

5. Epic Ideas & Imagination

Once you have creative confidence, you begin to experience epic idea creation (called "ideation") and crackling imagination. Your thoughts soar high in the sky like they're on a magic carpet ride. You see things differently in the world, and this creates a steady stream of new ideas in your mind. This confidence gives you the freedom to be bold with your assumptions. Grand in your thinking. Decisive in your plans. You walk around wide-eyed with wonder and *knowing* with courage.

Companies crave creativity from their superstar employees, and for good reason. It improves the bottom line by fostering innovation. That means creativity can boost your life, too. According to *The Creative Dividend,* Adobe asked Forrester Consulting to investigate how creativity can impact business outcomes. Forrester's study concluded that...

> *Companies that embrace creativity outperform peers and competitors on key business performance indicators, including revenue growth, market share, and talent acquisition.*

So think of it like this. When you have more ideas and a bigger imagination, you have more opportunities to increase your income, improve your relationships, and enjoy your life more.

I went from having no idea what I'd do to attract the abundance I wanted, to writing ten romance novels in a year. Now, when I wake up in the morning, I see life in radical new colors, shapes, and ways. I cock my head like a dog when I do things, curious, wondering if there are other ways, newer perspectives. I look forward to opposing opinions, meeting people of all walks of life, and exploring new angles to living.

This makes a creative life. It's weird. It's tantalizing. It breeds creativity, epic feelings, and an incredible sense of control, yet out-of-control, too, in a fun, exciting kind of way. It's like being strapped into a roller coaster, which keeps you feeling safe, but riding down hills and whipping around turns and twisty-loops, which is exhilarating! I gotta say... *Damn, it's SO fun living this way! Creativity for the win!*

The Wine Self-Talk scripts in Part II will help you improve your imagination and boost your confidence through creativity. Wine helps, but strictly speaking, it's not required. The process works. I now constantly walk around with a notepad or my phone, with the Notes app always open, ready to record ideas, because they pour out of me throughout the day, every day. Even when I'm working on something else, my creative engine keeps on cranking things out —*boom, boom, boom*—and my performance goes through the roof, as my brain gets saturated in a cauldron of rich neurochemistry... endorphins, serotonin, and dopamine. *Yum!* These light up my brain, and it feels awesome every time it happens. You feel bigger than life, like you've got meaning, purpose, and direction. It's amazing.

6. Sparkling Health

As I've mentioned, creativity decreases stress and anxiety, and this helps boost your health and well-being. When you're in a creative state, when you're feeling that *flow*, it boosts your mood and can even slow your heart rate. Calm takes over your soul, but you're still amped up with an excited energy, which keeps you going, shining and sparkling.

One of the reasons it all feels so good is because of dopamine, the "feel-good" chemical that motivates you to keep going and going. It's actually secreted in your brain *when you set goals*. And then, your brain continues to secrete it each time you take steps toward those goals. So the very fact that you're holding this book in your hands represents a goal of yours, because you seek the benefits of reading it.

And it also feels good when you make progress, such as completing a chapter, because you're taking a step toward your goal of finishing the book and starting the Wine Self-Talk. Pretty cool, huh? Now that you know how your brain's dopamine reward system works, you can be on the lookout for other goals and progress in your life, and make little rules with yourself to game the system (like defining what counts as a goal, and what counts as progress), to make yourself feel little blips of feel-goodness... *squirt, squirt, squirt.*

With this improved mood and state of well-being, having more creativity in your life can help with depression and anxiety. Because dopamine is like a natural anti-depressant. You're relaxed when you're being creative. When you're donning your creative hat, and in that magical flow state, you reduce the chatter in your mind, and worries and anxieties just kind of melt away. Like when you're cold from being out in the snow, and you step inside a warm house, feeling safe and toasty.

I had never realized how intricately woven stress, relaxation, and creativity are. You see, when stress is up, relaxation is down (of course), and that means creativity is down. But when relaxation is up, creativity is up. This makes sense now, but it wasn't obvious. It's no wonder I could never write good stories when I was stressed. My mind just didn't work as well.

As it happens, all of this is very important for the long-term health of your brain. According to CBS News, a study conducted by the Mayo Clinic reported that,

> *Engaging in a creative hobby helped reduce the risk of dementia and preserve memory... Participants who engaged in artistic hobbies such as painting, drawing, or sculpture, in both middle and old age, were 73 percent less likely to develop mild cognitive impairment than those who didn't.*

An article at Silver Sherpa reported on the work of behavioral neurologist Luis Fornazzari, stating,

> *My team discovered that the brain anatomy of musicians differed from others. As the musicians developed their skills and talent, they built special neural networks that were much more resistant to the effects of stroke, degeneration, and even traumatic brain injury... Art has a long-term positive effect on the brain.*

Now, you might be thinking, *But I don't play a musical instrument, Kristen!*

Well, you can start! In fact, once you've fully embraced what this whole book is about, the prospect of undertaking some massive goal —like learning to play a musical instrument, or learning a foreign language—these are not daunting, *they're exciting!*

And this is one of the ways you can use your Wine Self-Talk: using self-talk to inspire and encourage the desire to learn new things. Perhaps you don't play an instrument now, but you can absolutely customize your Wine Self-Talk scripts to focus on that goal. And, of course, this is not limited to music. It can help you muster the enthusiasm to embark on any new creative journey. Dancing, cooking, sculpting, graphic design, acting, writing, programming, and so much more!

~

The point of this book is to help you unleash your creativity to live a more magical life. It is to help you see the connection between stress and creativity, and it's to help you use this ritual to relax and build up your creative thought processes... your creativity muscle. Your inner genius.

And that's what all of the scripts in Part II focus on... different aspects of making your life magical by exploring and unleashing your wildly creative source. In *Coffee Self-Talk*, I provide a more general-purpose, well-rounded list of pre-made self-talk scripts, ranging from health and longevity, to abundance and success, to scripts for finding love, relationships, and parenting. But with *Wine Self-Talk,* our goal is to boost your creativity as an integral ingredient to magical living. I want to repeat... *being creative feels like magic*. Truly. When your brain makes connections with seemingly unconnected things, it feels like something *is happening*, an almost supernatural feeling. And this can all be yours by sitting down with a glass of wine and reading your scripts.

CHAPTER 4

WINE SELF-TALK

> *Make an empty space in any corner of your mind, and creativity will instantly fill it.*
>
> — Dee Hock

When I ventured into being a writer and an entrepreneur, I craved a process for incubating ideas, being inspired, feeling both magical and empowered at the same time. I've come a long way in my creativity, and it's all because of my self-talk.

It was an interesting journey. I came from having a Type-A, perfectionist, crack-the-whip mentality. Back then, creativity seemed like this airy-fairy, vaguely useless quality, unless I needed somebody to design an ad or a book cover. I mostly associated creativity with artists, and I didn't know many artists, but the ones I did know all seemed to be struggling to make a living. There were a few exceptions, friends of my husband who were concept artists for video game companies, or who did visual effects in Hollywood, but that seemed so far from my reality, it didn't really seem relevant. To me, "artists" were more like that second cousin you only see at weddings, who dreams of becoming a singer but isn't very good at it.

So that was my view on creativity. Pretty negative.

Man oh man, have I done a complete 180! On the other side of this journey, I've emerged more open-minded, more fascinated, more imaginative, and, most importantly, *way more creative myself*.

The trick was to somehow create a process that led to more of these creative flashes, to somehow build a breeding ground for my creativity to flourish. Using self-talk was the key to the kingdom. Gone are the days of waiting for inspiration, hoping and praying it will come. Waiting to be "in the mood." I'm always in the mood now. With self-talk, I've added creativity to my self-image, my identity. Meaning it's now a part of who I am. I've made creativity feel welcome, so instead of tiptoeing around the edges of my mind, now it bursts onto the scene, center stage, in the spotlight of my attention.

As I've mentioned, the first time I did this was using Coffee Self-Talk, to "talk myself" into becoming a novelist. But I use my daily Coffee Self-Talk to address all areas of my life—from happiness, to fitness, to parenting, to financial matters—and I wanted to carve out a special time, a ritual dedicated specifically to fueling my creative fire.

Wine Self-Talk fit the bill perfectly.

It's a weekly ritual where I relax my mind... I open it *waaaay* up. I'll go through the steps in detail in the next chapter, but here's the short version: I sit in my comfortable loveseat filled with pillows. I have my special journal by my side, along with my creativity totem: a beautiful, pink, Italian fountain pen. Literally, *a font of creativity*. I take a sip of wine, and I let the taste, the essence, the vapors, waft through my nose, anchoring the process in my soul, as though creative tendrils are taking root in my mind.

I then start reading my Wine Self-Talk script. Unlike my more energetic morning ritual, I speak the words softly, gently, almost like an incantation. My Wine Self-Talk scripts are special scripts filled with affirmations that are designed to boost my creativity to other-worldly levels. I use words and phrases that crack open my mind and allow the white-hot light of inspiration to blast in at all angles. My confidence gets a jolt, sitting up straight, like, *Hey! We mean business!*

The next part is subtle, hard to explain... but at this stage, I allow my lifelong obsession with *the known* (all the things I think I'm certain about)... this part of my mind softens, loosens its grip, so that I might waltz gently with the *unknown*. My eyes twinkle with curiosity. With possibility. I am open to learning new things. New ways of being me. I am open to *reimaging everything*. Not just in the world, but in myself.

And the flow begins.

Sometimes I jot down a note or two. Sometimes I write furiously. Sometimes, I just close my eyes, and let it wash through me, speaking to me, until it's finished saying whatever it wants to say.

~

The inspiration or solution I seek does not always appear in a single Wine Self-Talk session. And that's fine. Your inner genius, your creative source, is its own boss! You are opening the door for it, letting it know that it is welcome, appreciated, and loved.

Sometimes I do see immediate results. Less so when I first started doing this, more so now. Maybe I'm looking to solve a particular problem, or perhaps I have a book idea, but I don't know what to make the title, or what direction to take the story. So I plant seeds during my Wine Self-Talk, tailoring the words and affirmations to whatever I'm working on, such as:

The most amazing book titles come to me easily.
I have an abundance of ideas for excellent book titles.
I am a creative genius when it comes to naming my books.
My book titles immediately grab people's attention.

Sometimes I'm struck with inspiration, right then and there, during my Wine Self-Talk session. Those sessions border on orgasmic... I have to stop reading my script to write down the ideas.

Other times, it can take a few sessions of planting seeds and keeping myself open to the universe, and to my intuition. And then, suddenly, an idea may come to the fore, as though my inner genius has been working on it in the background. I might be riding in the car a week later, and suddenly, the answer strikes me from out of the blue. *Eureka!* I grab my phone and dictate notes.

And other times, the answer I receive from my inner genius is more subtle. Inspiration, like a living thing, whispers into my ear, giving me shivers, and I turn my eyes to it, curious. *"Oh, hello, that's an interesting thought. Shall we discuss?"*

The Wine Self-Talk Ritual is about opening your focus and relaxing, and teaching your body and mind what it feels like to exist with an unwound, beautiful, open-flow state, as often as possible. The process is relaxing and enjoyable, which is key to sustaining a creative mind long-term. And, over time, you train yourself to be able to think like this with the snap of your fingers because you'll have trained your brain to switch to *creative mode* on demand, whenever you want, once you know what it feels like, and once you do it enough times.

I've mentioned the term, *open focus*. What does that feel like? What does it mean? It's an experience, you know the one, where you're looking straight ahead, but instead of paying attention to the center of your field of vision, you broaden your attention to include the periphery. Your peripheral vision has a softness to it. Less detail, and less vibrant color. When you do this, your awareness is opening up, like a flower. It's the opposite of tunnel vision. Opening your mental focus feels the same way. You widen your mental gaze, relax, and welcome ideas from all around you.

Try this now... put down your book, and look straight ahead. Now widen your attention so that you notice the periphery, the outer edges. Without moving your eyes, what objects can you name from the periphery of your visual field? Notice that there's less detail in the periphery, like everything is softer. It's *this* feeling, this broader, softer focus, that you want to relax into when you're thinking creatively, when you're receiving ideas from your inner genius. This *soft focus* is how you let novel ideas know it's safe to come out and play. It's like a sixth sense, this softening of your mind. Blurring the edges of your reality.

> *Out on the edge, you see all kinds of things you can't see from the center. Big, undreamed-of things—the people on the edge see them first.*
>
> — Kurt Vonnegut

Why Wine?

One of my passions is biohacking, and I love experimenting with different foods, supplements, vitamins, and legal drugs. I use caffeine strategically. I also use L-theanine, the amino acid in green tea that helps people relax. I have explored smart drugs like modafinil. Altering cognitive processes, in search of upgrading my performance, is playtime to me. So the idea of biohacking with wine? *Hell yeah, baby!*

I'm not alone in this pursuit. Artists and musicians, as a subculture, are known for experimenting with mind-altering substances, both legal and illegal, in the pursuit of expanding their creativity. Ernest Hemingway is often attributed with saying, "Write drunk, edit sober," which is fascinating advice, as though he's implicitly referring to two different parts of his brain that perform two very different tasks.

As it happens, Hemingway did drink excessively, but he never said such a thing. In fact, he felt precisely the opposite. Here's what Hemingway said about drinking and writing:

> *Jeezus Christ! Have you ever heard of anyone who drank while he worked? You're thinking of Faulkner... and I can tell right in the middle of a page when he's had his first one.*

Ya gotta love Hemingway.

To be clear, I'm not advocating that you *get drunk* during your Wine Self-Talk ritual. Or even tipsy. In fact, I recommend that you stop drinking *as soon as you feel the effect* from the alcohol. Ride that smooth, relaxed sensation while you complete your ritual. At least, that's what I do, because any more wine, and I get very tired, very fast, and my creativity does a nosedive.

You know your body best, so use your best judgment here. You may wish to have a longer session. You may wish to journal for an hour after doing your self-talk. You may already be drinking a glass or two of wine most evenings and have a higher tolerance.

Wine can help boost your creativity, but always remember that alcohol is also toxic, so try to strike the right balance for you. It's all about moderation. In particular, be careful about becoming dependent. Wine can help *train* you to access the creative part of your brain —like training wheels on a bike. But you don't ever want to find yourself *needing* wine to access your inner genius. Wine is not required for this ritual, and once you've become accustomed to tapping into your inner genius, wine should not be required to continue doing it.

Good news! According to Dr. Weil,

> *Alcohol can be a benign and useful social/recreational drug that may benefit overall health by reducing stress and the risk of cardiovascular disease. Moderation and awareness are the keys to using it successfully and protecting yourself from harm and the risk of dependence.*

There you go. Doctor approved—*yay*. Dr. Weil concurs with my comments on moderation, and the research behind the creativity and problem-solving benefits of drinking wine support this view. Only a small amount of alcohol will deliver the desired effects. Once you have too much, you can experience the opposite reaction: mental fogginess, tiredness, and sluggishness. Creativity under these circumstances can be like trying to climb out of quicksand. Blindfolded. Hands tied.

There's a lot of research linking alcohol with creativity. Dr. Mathias Benedek published a paper, *Creativity on Tap? Effects of Alcohol Intoxication on Creative Cognition* (Consciousness & Cognition, 2017), in which he says that a small drink can help with certain elements of creativity, from creative writing to brainstorming ideas among business executives.

Dr Mathias' research team found that the alcohol drinkers "exceeded in a creative thinking task," and he offers the following possible explanation: First, when you drink alcohol, you tend to have less focus and "cognitive control," which can be extremely useful for creativity, because, when you're too tunnel-focused on a problem, you can't generate any peripheral, creative solutions. You can be so fixated on the details of a challenge that your mind gets stuck in a rut, going in circles, spinning on a merry-go-round.

Alcohol *makes it more difficult* for you to stay focused on the problem. Which helps you approach the problem from different angles. Inspiration is a lot easier to come by when you let down your hyper-focus guard.

Our brains have a thing called *working memory*, which keeps our thoughts about the task at hand front and center, thereby keeping out any extraneous thoughts and distractions. This is important when working on problems that require concentration. But it's not so helpful when you want to think outside the box. Working memory prevents you from moving beyond what you already know, and it can stifle your ability to imagine something in new and novel ways.

This is where alcohol can help. According to Jennifer Wiley, Ph.D., *"Alcohol manipulates focus."* This is good for helping you get out of a rut, or break through when you're creatively burned out. It's great for opening your mind to answers that you wouldn't be as likely to come up with when sober. Which is not what you want when filing your taxes, no matter how creative you want to get with your deductions.

For out-of-the box tasks, you want taffy-like, stretchy thinking. And that's why we're pairing wine with your self-talk... to create a superior experience.

And finally, it must be said... drinking wine just *feels good.* I mean, *hello*, sipping a little vino, chilling in an armchair, doing your self-talk, a little smile on your lips.

Sounds nice, right?

It's not your imagination. According to a study from the University of California, San Francisco, drinking alcohol releases endorphins in the brain. You know, more of those feel-good chemicals.

What? Wine makes you feel good? Yes, shocking, I know. I could've told the scientists that and saved them a bunch of fuss, haha. Still, I suppose knowing that wine might increase the endorphins zooming around in my brain is a nice, sciency reason for me to open a bottle of Pinot. Combine "wine for creativity and feeling good" with "feel-good self-talk focused on creativity" and...

BAM!... Creativity unleashed!

Let's get started.

CHAPTER 5

HOW TO DO WINE SELF-TALK: THE RITUAL

The world is but a canvas to the imagination.

— Henry David Thoreau

Here are the steps to your Wine Self-Talk ritual.

You'll need two things:

1. A glass of wine (or other beverage)
2. Your chosen self-talk script

Your choice of wine can change by the season, or by your taste, or what you have on hand. And remember, you don't need wine to do this; creativity can be unleashed by the self-talk alone! But tying it to a drink, alcoholic or otherwise, intensifies the connection, anchoring it, making it more special. That's what rituals do.

Your script can be one from Part II of this book, or a modified version of one of them, or a script that you write yourself. (See instructions, later in this chapter.)

Find a special place to sit down. This could be in your living room, curled up on the couch. I like to dim the lights a bit or have a fire going, if possible, season permitting. I think of it like I'm on a date, courting my creativity.

Step 1: Believe

It's time to plant the seeds to unleash your creativity. The first step is acknowledging how amazing your life will be with more creativity. Commit and devote yourself to this process. Believe in it.

Step 2: Take a Sip, and Read Your Script 1 to 2 Times

Take your script, and read through it slowly, once or twice. Enjoy a sip of your wine occasionally, feeling the sensation of the liquid on your tongue, and pay attention to the nuanced smell and flavors. Notice the warming sensation as you swallow the wine.

If possible, read your script out loud. Above, I mentioned that you can think of this ritual like you're on a date with your creativity, and if you read your script out loud, it's as if you're talking to your inner creative self. You're *engaging* with creativity. In the beginning, some people don't feel comfortable reading their scripts out loud, and that's ok. They feel self-conscious, or a bit silly. But trust me, it gets easier once you've done it a couple of times. Eventually, you won't even think about it. And reading out loud, even a whisper, makes the entire process more fun and gives it a stronger impact. You're not only reading the lines with your eyes, but your ears are hearing it. Your mouth is feeling the words. You're involving more sense modalities, more regions of your brain.

Step 3: Close the Book

Once you've read through your script once or twice, close the book and set it aside. Look off into the distance, or at nothing in particular.

Allow your gaze to soften, letting the seeds of creativity take root inside you. Enjoy the feeling of knowing that you're taking action, setting yourself up for success, opening your mind and heart to more connections and bigger possibilities. Enjoy the relaxed, blissful ride.

Step 4: Journal (Optional)

If you'd like, you might want to keep a journal or notebook handy. If the mood strikes, jot down any ideas or inspiration that come to you at this time. It can be simple words that pop into your mind, or multiple pages... whatever you want. Or you might be inspired to doodle, or draw, or write large, decorative words in big, fancy fonts. Anything that helps you record what you're experiencing at the moment, whether it's ideas, feelings, solutions, or even just words that vaguely describe your emotions.

You're still keeping your mind wide open, letting all ideas flow through you, channeling them, whatever they are. It can be surreal, almost dream-like. Simply capture the feelings and thoughts, and jot down any notes that come to mind. Don't judge or self-edit, just go with the flow... you never know where things might lead.

All that said, this journaling step is optional. There won't always be something you feel like writing down. And remember that these seeds are only just now taking root. Sometimes you will have a flash of inspiration right there, during your Wine Self-Talk ritual, but oftentimes it will come later, unexpectedly. An *aha* moment. Other times, the insight will be more subtle, and you make a gentle connection that makes you shrug and nod your head like, *"Oh yeah, that'll work. Cool."*

There is no time pressure for this process. No constraints. And the more you open up your mind to the *creative source* inside of you, the more the inspiration and creativity will start to show themselves in your day-to-day world.

Creativity Starter Questions for Your Wine Self-Talk Ritual

Write to me at Kristen@KristenHelmstetter.com for some free goodies (be sure to mention "Wine Self-Talk Goodies"). The goodies come in a PDF that contains a printable version of the scripts in this book, a bonus chapter, and a list of *Creativity Starter Questions* that are designed to prompt your creative thinking.

When doing your Wine Self-Talk session, if you find yourself desiring a little creativity boost, or some pre-session warmup inspiration, then pull out the questions, and start writing answers to them in your journal or notebook. This is a fun and easy way to get the creativity ball rolling during your Wine Self-Talk ritual.

How to Write Your Own Wine Self-Talk Scripts

> *Enthusiasm is excitement with inspiration, motivation, and a pinch of creativity.*
>
> — Bo Bennett

In Part II of this book, you'll see the chapters divided into what I call *lessons*, and each one has its own Wine Self-Talk script.

When you read a script, if you like it the way it is, then by all means, use it.

Or perhaps you like some of the lines, but you'd like to change or add some of your own affirmations. Then by all means, do that. The exact words you use are important for maximizing your self-talk's impact. You want words that stir feelings in your heart and create vivid pictures in your mind.

For this reason, I highly encourage you to write your own scripts, too, if you have any interest in customizing your experience. I'm now going to teach you the fundamentals of how I write my scripts. You'll want to get a journal with blank lines, or simply a pad of paper. I prefer a journal or notebook because I like to keep my self-talk scripts in their own dedicated place. And I like having different notebooks for different rituals, which is why I offer a blank-lined journal for *Coffee Self-Talk,* and a separate one for *Pillow Self-Talk,* and another for *Wine Self-Talk*. That said, any journal will do.

I also love colored pens, and stickers, and highlighters. I jazz it up and get playful with it, making my inner fourth grader squeal in delight.

Or you can type these into your laptop, or an app on your phone such as *Notes* (iPhone) or *Evernote*. I have a whole group of notes in the Notes app, for all my different self-talk scripts, so I always have them with me.

Decide whatever works best for you, and you can always change it later. Be advised, however, that inspiration strikes at all times of the day, and you want to make sure you have some system in place to capture the sparks of genius when they happen.

Some Tips

I'll offer some quick tips here for writing your own scripts for your Wine Self-Talk ritual. If you'd like to really dig into writing your own, please see *Coffee Self-Talk*, where I cover the topic in detail.

"I" Versus "You"

I recommend always writing your self-talk in first person. For example:

I create from the heart, and when I do this, ideas flow through me effortlessly.

When you read or speak "I" instead of "you," the words will feel more relevant, like you're receiving instructions, which is exactly what's happening.

Present Tense

I write my affirmations in the present tense. I don't use the future tense, such as, "I will do such and such," because stating things in the present tense makes them seem real to your subconscious, as if they have already happened. This is accompanied by a feeling of gratitude and awe.

Script Length

Most of my scripts range from 15 to 25 lines each, and I'll read through a script two or three times in a single session. Sometimes, when I really focus on a single affirmation, conjuring up a big, vivid picture inside my mind, I might only go through the script one time, but it might take me five minutes to get through it.

Jazzing It Up

I mentioned colored pens and stickers above, and I do something similar if I have my script in my phone or on my laptop. I'll add pictures, or emojis, or bold print, or italics to emphasize different things. Your mind is most successful at helping you create your magical life when it has a vivid picture to work from. For me, the better the picture, the easier it is to envision... and the easier it is to make it real.

Big vs. Small Sentences — Flowery vs. Punchy

You'll see that my affirmations range in size and length from one to the next. That's intentional. I mix up the rhythm to the reading, so that sometimes there's an affirmation that's long and flowery—*la dee da*—and other times, it's short and punchy—*bam!*

Sometimes I make it a little poetic with some rhyming. If you are new to writing your own self-talk scripts, then you might find yourself starting off with very basic affirmations, and that's just fine. I still include a lot of simple, straightforward affirmations—like, *I am worthy, I am loved, I am amazing*—and you'll see these sprinkled throughout the scripts in Part II. Those simple self-talk lines are just as powerful. But you'll also sometimes see that I go *way out there,* with words and phrases that might make you do a double take. There are a few reasons for this. Not only do the words and phrases create a more distinct picture in your mind, but also:

1. It's more fun! It tickles the artist in me.
2. It makes you pause. By catching your attention, you typically have a stronger feeling from reading it.

Themes & Repetition

My scripts always have a theme of worthiness and self-love underlying everything. Having a sense of worthiness is essential for all of the other affirmations to work. And having this sense of worthiness is what makes for having the greatest life experience.

In addition to the affirmations about self-love and self-worth, there is the obvious *creativity* theme for the scripts in this book, and so you'll see lines about creativity in every script. Scripts can be a mishmash of different topics, but keeping a script focused on one theme, and reading 20-some lines about this same idea—just written different ways—really makes it take root deep inside your mind. It keeps firing and firing, and then wiring more strongly inside your brain.

The repetition is very important, so embrace it. Television ads are a perfect example of how effective repetition is at lodging something in your memory. They either repeat things over and over in the ad, or they show you the ad repeatedly. We're doing the same thing here, so have fun with it!

Welcome to Your New Creative Life

Today, you're going to start creating a new creative life (or when you first do your Wine Self-Talk session, if that's not today).

You're going to:

1) Decide you're worthy and capable of the most incredible creativity. Claim it! This decision *allows the process to start*. If you don't feel this now, don't worry, just keep saying it, and pretend you feel it. It will start to sink in, I promise!

2) Believe it's possible. Belief makes it happen faster. Don't worry if you don't believe it yet, such as if you've never thought of yourself as creative... you will by the time you do the ritual a few times. Just stick with it.

3) Show up and do it. Commit to yourself that you're going to do this fun ritual. I mean, it *really is* super fun! And then watch as strange, cool, and incredibly neat things and creative ideas start to flow through your mind and your life.

You are capable of magic.

> *Inventions, great musical compositions, poetry, fiction, and all other ideas for original accomplishment come from the subconscious. Give it the thought, and keep it going with a deep-rooted desire, and you will get results.*
>
> — Dana Sleeth

PART II

WINE SELF-TALK SCRIPTS

CHAPTER 6

WINE SELF-TALK SCRIPT: WIDE-EYED, UNINHIBITED THINKING

> *There is a fountain of youth: It is your mind, your talents, the creativity you bring to your life, and the lives of people you love.*
>
> — Sophia Loren

"Hey, Greg, crazy idea here," I say, with last night's Arizona Cardinals football game on my mind.

"Hit me," he says.

"Ok. Story idea for a sports mystery novel... you know how football teams have a water boy on the sidelines who squirts Gatorade into the players' mouths?"

"Yeah, I guess."

"Well," I continue, "what if an evil antagonist filled those bottles for one of the teams with something like valerian or melatonin, and the players get all sleepy on the field, falling over like dominos, and sleeping on the benches?" My hands shake with excitement.

He laughs. "That is crazy. I like it."

Three years ago, I never would never have come up with such a weird idea, let alone tell another human about it. But my life is different now. I've come to realize that I get the most creative bang for the buck when my thinking is completely uninhibited. Embracing all of my wide-eyed wonder. Asking a constant stream of questions that start with *"What if...?"*

What if there were a magical place with skies filled with flying dolphins? What if the world were run by obedient robots, but then one day, one of them fell in love with its human? What if the villain drugged an entire football team with sleeping potion mid-game?

What if I had so many ideas that their quality didn't even matter? Because I could choose the diamonds among them, the best 2–3 ideas out of a hundred, and discard the rest, knowing there would always be more where those came from?

And, oh my... it's so much fun. Having fun is such an important part of life. Allowing yourself to let go relaxes you, and relaxation is the grease that lets your brain's creativity gears spin freely. When you're having fun, you don't judge. And when you don't judge, you open up the floodgates of possibility. If you're having fun, you know you're headed in the right direction. You're looking for that loosey-goosey feeling, a face flushed with fascination, and eyes wide open in wonder.

Just like a child.

Want to know the real secret to creativity?

I'll tell you. It's shockingly simple. The secret is combining *ordinary things in unordinary ways*. Skies and dolphins. Robots and love. Football and valerian.

See how easy that is?

And the weirder, the better. But mostly, you don't even worry about weirdness level. Instead, focus on *volume*. The *number* of new ideas, new combinations. And then you throw most of them away, and keep a few of them to work with, now or in the future.

Creative ideas come from recycling, and reinventing, and salvaging things in your current environment. For me, herbal medicine is always on my mind, hence the valerian. And we had just watched a football game. Boom. *Intersection!* New idea. That's creativity.

Because I allowed it.

I set myself up for it.

I told myself that uninhibited thinking is where it all begins.

And that means *no rules!*

Young children do this naturally. I remember my daughter taking yarn and pencils, and toilet paper rolls, and paperclips, and empty egg cartons, and making things out of them, connecting them with Scotch tape. I have no idea what the creations were. But that doesn't matter. In fact, that's the whole point. They weren't anything that has a name. They were something brand new. Something that had never existed before. Creating *new* things by connecting existing things. That's creativity.

Kids have an *innate desire* to create. An instinct. As though making things is what makes us human, and most of us have had our natural creativity pounded out of us by the time we're adults. But we all still have an innate need, deep down inside of us, to look at our surroundings and see what new things we can make from them.

Why are kids so much better at this?

For starters, kids—especially young kids—don't fear embarrassment or failure. They *learn* to fear failure. They *learn* embarrassment, as a by-product of learning how to fit in. They also aren't preoccupied with stress, wondering where their next meal is coming from, or whether they'll be able to pay the rent next month. Still, there's something so pure and magical about the way children see a table full of items with an excited sparkle in their eyes. They can't help themselves... MUST. MAKE. THINGS!

Me? Not so long ago, I would see a table of things as a bunch of junk that needed to be put away.

But I've learned better. I've used self-talk to wire creativity into my brain so it's more of a default way of thinking, rather than something I have to expend effort to do. And one way to help you enter the creative realm with ease is to practice living through the eyes of a child.

Embody your inner child's self. In this state, we see new product ideas in the clouds overhead. We're free to imagine what it would be like if we added cinnamon to our lime vinaigrette, drizzled over a romaine salad topped with sliced bananas. Or we try on our cowgirl boots with Nike gym shorts! (Hey, I didn't say every idea would be a hit, but that salad was damn tasty!) We boldly connect things and have fun while doing it, giggling at the craziness that sometimes whizzes through our minds.

What if this?

What if that?

What if? What if? What if?

That all sounds great! How do you get there? *Self-talk*, my love! Show up to life with the best words and thoughts about yourself and your creativity, and just kick back, and watch the magic start to happen. You will, indeed, be wide-eyed when the most crazy-cool ideas and solutions come to you. And you'll start to feel more relaxed about things that might have previously upset you and kept your creativity tucked away.

Remember, creativity behaves like a muscle. The more you work it, the stronger it gets. The more often you fire and wire creativity in your brain, the easier it is to tap into on demand, because it becomes your default way of thinking. It even becomes part of your identity!

Do as Earl Nightingale says, for spurring creativity:

> *Think combination, association, adaptation, substitution, magnification, and rearrangement.*

At first, do this every time you want to create, or when you want inspiration or innovation. Later on, you'll start to do it without trying, in situations where you didn't even realize that creativity was needed. Turns out, creativity is a lot more useful than most people realize. What can you modify that you never dreamed of modifying because "it works fine" the way it is? When you eyeball life through this creativity lens, you can almost feel your brain squishing, and moving, and changing inside your skull. It's in there *exercising!* Getting buff. And you'll be blown away by the ideas that can come of it!

Take a deep breath...

It's time to welcome uninhibited thinking and wide-eyed wonder into your life. It's time to let creativity come out to play. As Edward de Bono says,

> *Creativity involves breaking out of established patterns in order to look at things in a different way.*

So let's get some self-talk going to support that. The following script is designed to increase your relaxation, increase your fun, and take full advantage of uninhibited thinking for making connections and unleashing the creative genius that's already inside you.

Wine Self-Talk Script: Wide-Eyed, Uninhibited Thinking

I am worthy of creativity. It seeks me, and I seek it.

I sense creativity all around me. I open my arms and welcome it into my life.

I see life through the eyes of my inner child. I giggle, snicker, and scrunch my face with excitement.

Inspiration finds me everywhere, and it happens naturally, because I am open to everything.

I make room for my creativity to come out and play. I always ask, "What if? What if? What if?"

Inventive ideas are brewing and stewing in my mind at this very moment. I am confident!

I am soooo relaxed, and my mind is wide open for making connections.

I love my life, and life loves me. I'm so worthy and lucky!

My creations and ideas are meaningful. They glimmer like stars in the sky.

I show up to my life, bright-eyed and bushy-tailed, ready for fun, excitement, and originality.

I know that it is safe to follow my truth into the land of wide-eyed playtime.

My creativity is on a playground in my mind, running around and making rad connections. Woohoo, this is fun!

I can look anywhere and be inspired to connect unrelated things into something brand new.

I choose confidence. I choose joy. I choose rainbow-colored, brilliant living.

I have daily playdates with my creativity. It's always there, willing and waiting for me to join hands with it.

My soul is filled with wonder and awe. Everywhere I look, I notice opportunities, because I'm free to believe.

My thinking is uninhibited, so I make the coolest connections.

I am healthy, vibrant, and I feel amazing.

I'm gifted with uninhibited thinking and a universe-sized sense of wonder.

I exercise my creativity muscle, and I can feel it getting stronger every day.

Ideas flow through me. They're always there for the taking.

Ideas are cheap and come easily to me. I have thousands of them, an endless supply.

Whenever I'm faced with a new situation, new ways of dealing with it come to me effortlessly.

Every day, in every way, I'm more and more creative.

I am relaxed and enjoying every moment right now, every word, and every juicy thought.

Creativity Tip: Turn Off All Distractions

When you're doing your Wine Self-Talk, I recommend you turn notifications *off* on your phone, and that you physically locate yourself away from your computer and the television (or turn them off). If you like, play some relaxing music without lyrics in the background. Or perhaps get a water feature, like a desktop fountain, for added relaxation. Or just sit in complete silence. This is to avoid any possible distractions, so your brain stays open-focused and uninhibited in its creative flow.

CHAPTER 7

WINE SELF-TALK SCRIPT: CREATING FROM THE HEART

> *You have to be burning with an idea, or a problem, or a wrong that you want to right. If you're not passionate enough from the start, you'll never stick it out.*
>
> — Steve Jobs

Creating things from the heart... *ahhh*, there's nothing more enjoyable. When you create from the heart, it's like saturating your efforts with pixie dust. Golden ideas start to flow from your mind. It's easier to tap into creativity, and your inspiration explodes. This is because creating from the heart is real. It's pure. And because of this, you experience elevated feelings, and believe in yourself.

This is how I feel about spreading my love of self-talk and its power to others. I look around, and I see too many people not living up to their potential, not happy. Drifting, or lost.

It doesn't have to be that way! We *can* live more magnificent lives when we spruce them up with creativity. This chapter is about creating from the heart, regardless of what kind of creating inspires you.

Creating from the heart is like making a home-cooked meal. If you have a choice between cooking from scratch versus microwaved frozen food, the home-cooked meal is galaxies better.

That's what you want to do. Approach creativity with a home-cooked mindset, like you're cooking with love. Exploring and pursuing from your heart. You want to be wide open, arms stretched out, available to receive all the creativity coming your way. From this, you see what lights you up the most. When truly creating from the heart, your eyes fire, you tingle inside, and you feel a sense of destiny. It makes you want to move, move, move.

This is creating from the heart. You might come up with the nuts and bolts with your mind, but you fill in the rest with your heart. You might be surprised at how easy this is once you're doing Wine Self-Talk. Something totally unexpected might come from left field, crashing into an idea that spiraled in from behind. It's amazing. Be open to it all. Be open to possibilities, and have confidence that it's all there for the taking. You just have to believe, and see yourself as a creative person.

That's exactly what happened for me when I became a romance author. Prior to my transformation, I didn't think I had a drop of novelist blood inside me. I thought the extent of my creativity was choosing which lipstick to wear. I delegated all creative projects to my husband, even if it meant telling bedtime stories to our daughter. Scratch that—*especially* when it meant telling her stories.

But one day, I was working out in the gym, and I added a few lines to my self-talk:

I am a prolific writer.
I am a creative genius.
I am filled with stories.
Writing novels is easy for me.

I snuck these lines into my self-talk like I sneak ground liver into a hamburger patty. I said my self-talk every day, and I ate my metaphorical liver every day.

Then, one day, some months later, something amazing happened.

I was sitting in my mom's backyard, surrounded by grapefruit and lemon trees, and the blazing Arizona sunshine. This was at the beginning of the pandemic. I suddenly had an idea for a story. It popped into my head, as though by magic. From out of the blue. I was so shocked, I turned around in my chair to see where the idea came from. Surely not from me, right?

But it was from me!

And once that floodgate opened, *holy shit...* more and more story ideas started coming to me. My confidence soared. I was on fire. *I still am!* My passion keeps me motivated. I wouldn't even consider stopping. I'm a snowball rolling down a hill, gathering momentum and ideas as I roll... making my life and creations bigger and bigger. My life will never be the same. And all this, after having lived over 40 years of never, ever once thinking of myself as a novelist.

From there, I just wrote, and wrote, and wrote. The words poured from me like an avalanche, five thousand, ten thousand, even twelve thousand words a day. Why? Because I loved what I was doing. I believed in my books and my creativity, knowing it would take me on an amazing journey. My heart was *all in*. And this made for the adventure of a lifetime.

You want to create from the heart. Not only does it motivate you and inspire you to continue working on your projects, but it also keeps you more open, more welcoming to new and crazy ideas. Tapping into your *inner genius*. Compare this to the alternative, such as work you feel "forced" to do.

Here's an example. Authors can write what they're passionate about, or they can do what's called "writing to market." Which means they see what's selling well, and they write something targeted to that market. Many authors do this, whipping out book after book without requiring inspiration. I respect that, but it doesn't sound magical. Or nearly as fun.

It sounds a lot like *work*.

I write about *things that inspire me*, and then I can write all day long. I don't require any daily inspiration to sit down and write, because I love what I'm doing... writing from the heart.

The following self-talk is to support you finding and becoming creative from your heart, in a natural, whole, heart-centered way. And to continue that inspiration over time, so you feel like you're floating down *Creativity River* in an inner-tube with ease and excitement. *Woohoo!*

Wine Self-Talk Script: Creating from the Heart

I love the ideas swirling and twirling in my heart. It is a safe place to find creativity.

I am a powerhouse of love, for myself and my ideas.

I create from the heart, and when I do this, ideas flow through me effortlessly.

I create art from the heart, and it's spectacular.

Ideas and inspiration rush through me, and I capture and record everything with verve and gusto. My motto is, "I'm onto something amazing!"

I can do anything I put my heart into.

I open my wings, spread them wide, and fly. I'm a creative soul. It's my nature. It comes easily to me. Watch me soar!

I am passionate about my projects, my art, my business, and my creativity.

I am worthy, so very, very worthy.

I am love, and I love sharing my creations with the world.

Gratitude for my raw creative powers makes me grin. I'm honored to have so much creativity inside me.

Original ideas and options fall into my lap constantly, because I set myself up to live a creative life. I follow my heart, and it always knows the way.

When I look into the mirror, I see that fresh ideas are bubbling inside me. They're dancing in my soul and juicing up my joy. I love my life!

I am comfy and confident inside my warm, creative, pulsing heart.

I am ready to be me, and that means I am free. Creating from my heart and filled with relaxed, comfortable ease.

The positive words that I speak to myself every day are firing and wiring in my brain, stirring up creations in my heart.

I ride my heart-driven passion like it's a powerful stallion. I'm free, fast, and bold.

I love myself. I love others. I love the world.

I am filled with ideas that make the world a better place.

I feel my aliveness in every moment. I breathe in marvelous ideas, and I breathe out creative expressions.

My life is amazing!

Creativity Tip: Carry an *Idea Notebook*

From here on out, pay attention to every new idea that comes to you. Whether big or small, notice any connection you make, any curious and sparkling questions that sweep through your mind.

A great way to help you do this is to have a special little notebook and pen that you carry with you everywhere you go, just for this purpose. Having it there, ready to accept your fun, crazy ideas, you can quickly jot down thoughts, or make doodles or sketches, whenever a flash of insight hits you. It also helps to get these interesting concepts and ideas out of your brain to make space for new ones.

The very act of slipping your *Idea Notebook* into your pocket or purse is like turning the light in your mind to *green for go*. You now have an official way to receive your creative genius, and your mind steps up to start banging stuff out. Your mind starts looking for opportunities to create. You'll find that you reach for your notebook more and more as the weeks and months go by, because your creativity muscle gets bigger and stronger.

Don't worry about understanding what every idea or connection means. The point isn't to interpret them, or even to do anything with them... not yet, anyway. The point is simply to record them, developing the *habit* of generating new ideas. Figuring out what to do with all this spewing of genius can come later. For now, just get it down on paper. The energy of creative expression that is tapping on your door. Open the door, and welcome it in.

CHAPTER 8

WINE SELF-TALK SCRIPT: BECOMING A PROBLEM-SOLVING NINJA

> *Chess masters don't evaluate all the possible moves. They discard 98 percent of the ones they could make, and then they focus on the best choice of the remaining lot. Wise practitioners in other fields recognize familiar patterns and put their creativity, improvisation, and skill toward the marginal cases.*
>
> — John Dickerson

To a certain brand of badass—the problem-solvers out there—problems are awesome. They're things we *get to solve*. Mathematicians aren't afraid of math problems, they devote their careers to solving them. To them, problems are fun. Solving them is *rewarding*.

And what about engineers? They love solving problems. That's basically what they do. Same goes for a lot of managers. And architects. And doctors. And lawyers.

When you think of yourself as a *problem-solver*, when that's part of your *identity*, everything around you becomes easier, because you become good at bending the world to your will. It's a superpower you can possess just by deciding to.

Problem? No problem.
Why? Because I'm a problem solver!

But it gets even better...

Good news: *Problems are actually great!*

So says Peter Diamandis, named one of the World's 50 Greatest Leaders by *Fortune* magazine. When he sees a big problem, giant hearts shoot out of his eyes, like Roger Rabbit swooning over Jessica Rabbit—*boinggg!*—because, when Peter sees a problem, he sees a gold mine. That's because the world's biggest problems are also the world's biggest business opportunities.

I like it. That's a good spin on problems.

So, the first rule is seeing problems as opportunities. *Check!*

Be ok with problems, and approach them with intrigue. *Check!*

And confidence.

Wait a sec... confidence? That one doesn't get a check so fast.

How can you approach problems with confidence?

Easy. You become a *Problem-Solving Ninja.* How do you become a Problem-Solving Ninja? Improve your problem-solving skills. How does one do that? Let's dive in.

First, let me whet your appetite with the benefits of becoming a Problem-Solving Ninja. You fashion strategies to solve long-term issues, you transform problems into dazzling opportunities, and you live a more magical life from all the reduced stress.

Turning into a Problem-Solving Ninja is one of the best benefits of living a creative life, but problems aren't usually what you think of when you think of creativity, right? The best way to understand this is simply to grasp that, when you're in a creative mindset, you make all kinds of wacky-awesome connections that you wouldn't normally do under a state of stress. Which means that people who get stressed out by problems actually shut down the part of the brain that's best equipped to deal with the situation. Whereas you, the Problem-Solving Ninja, not only *don't* get stressed, but you *actually enjoy this shit*, because it lights up your creative genius, and gives you tons of satisfaction when you fix whatever needed to be fixed.

Remember *The Wolf*, played by Harvey Keitel in the movie, *Pulp Fiction*? His job was to make problems disappear. When somebody had a problem, all they had to do was call him. The Wolf was a Problem-Solving Ninja, and you can be one, too. How? By doing what The Wolf did. His secret to solving problems? He remained extremely relaxed.

Relax & Let Go

Having a relaxed mindset allows your brain to make unique and clever connections, and it helps you get creative in the problem-solving process.

If you find yourself stuck when looking for the solution to a problem, sometimes the best approach is to step away from it for a while. Take a break. Or work on something else. This is also known as *task switching*, and it helps shake up your thought processes before you crash into a wall with exhaustion. When you go back-and-forth between tasks or projects, it allows you to reset your thinking. It helps your brain get out of ruts, and look in different directions for potential solutions. This often leads to seeing the situation from fresh, and sometimes, unusual angles.

Task switching also helps to relax you. You can pause to take a breath, knowing you'll come back to the issue later. And if you still can't figure it out on the second or third go, no problem. Put it to rest again.

The unknown can feel uncomfortable, but in the quest for creativity, stepping outside of your comfort zone is one of the goals. Because that's where the magic happens. When you relax and let go, your mind doesn't freeze up, it expands into new directions. It becomes open and happy. The more often you do it, the easier it gets to enter your creative zone, and unleashing this inner genius helps you solve all kinds of problems.

Seeing a Problem Backwards

One of the great paths to ingenuity is to see a problem backwards, as if it's already a solution to something else.

In the 1980s, the Japan Railways East company was digging a tunnel through a mountain to lay track for a high-speed bullet train. The problem was, the tunnel kept filling with water, melting snow runoff from the mountain above. The company's engineers struggled to find a solution to what seemed like an endless flood of water.

One day, a thirsty maintenance worker drank some of the water, and noticed that it tasted delicious. He suggested that the company bottle it and sell it!

The company did just that, placing vending machines for their bottled mineral water on over a thousand train station platforms. They later added fruit juice and iced tea, and within a decade, sales of their bottled beverages exceeded $50 million a year!

They turned the problem into something of value.

Scratching Your Own Itch

In startup culture, entrepreneurs, engineers, and tinkerers of all sorts have a concept called *scratching your own itch*. The idea is that you have an "itch" (a personal need), and you figure out a way to scratch it. And then, you reason that you're not the only one with that itch, so maybe other people will find it useful.

One evening in 2008, a young man attending a conference in Paris was unable to hail a taxi. He suddenly wished he could request a ride using his phone. The man's name was Travis Kalanick, and he started a little company you might have heard of. Today, Uber has a market cap of over $83 billion. *Now that's scratching your own itch!*

Dancing Your Way to Answers

Yes, dancing. Another way to amp up your creative-thinking for solving problems can be to dance. *Woo-hoo!* You might think it's a bit silly, but experts say that dancing has an impact on neural processing. But get this... the *type of dancing* changes the impact! If you want help with focused thinking, then dancing that's tightly structured is the ticket. Think: ballet. (*Yikes.*) However, when you want a more free-form mode of thinking, the creative kind, then you want something less constrained, like hip-hop. (*Phew.* That's more up my alley.)

Get Some ZZZ's

To improve your problem solving and creativity, get some sleep. In a study, psychologist Deidre Barrett, Ph.D., told her students to think about a problem before going to sleep. She discovered that they came up with solutions to the problems in their dreams! She found that half of the students reported having dreams that *addressed the specific problem* they focused on, and a quarter of them came up with *actual solutions* in their dreams.

In a study published in *Nature*, researchers found that participants who took a nap during their break when working on a long, boring math problem were more than twice as likely to figure out a better way to solve the problem, versus those who hadn't slept.

I mean, really! This stuff is low-hanging fruit... dancing, sleeping, and letting go to solve problems? *Sign me up!*

Remember! Problems Are Gorgeous Gifts

Problems are gifts, albeit strange gifts at first. But can you honestly say you didn't learn something from almost every problem you've ever had? Or that you didn't come out better, or wiser? Even if there was a situation that you think your life could've done well without, I challenge that. Even in that dark time, it *taught you more to appreciate the light in life.*

It all depends on how you look at things. Problems can always be viewed with rose-colored glasses. We grow much more from challenges than we do from living easy-ass lives. We appreciate more after coming through a trying time. We're stronger and smarter for having done it.

Problems are not bad. They are the steps that we take up the mountain of progress. Each problem we solve makes us a stronger, more badass, veteran Problem-Solving Ninja.

As the famous Latin saying goes,

Per aspera ad astra.
(Through hardships to the stars.)

And lots of the time, the best solutions to problems come from someplace unexpected. The following script is designed to help you tap into the inner source of problem-solving genius that we all possess.

> *Listen to anyone with an original idea, no matter how absurd it may sound at first. If you put fences around people, you get sheep. Give people the room they need.*
>
> — William McKnight, 3M President

Wine Self-Talk Script: Becoming a Problem-Solving Ninja

I see problems as exciting challenges, and I jump into them with gusto!

Every time a question comes to me, I ask a simple and powerful question, "What if?" And this always brings me new ideas.

I dance my way—jiggy, jiggy, pop!—to answers and solutions.

Wires cross in my brain, and these wires crackle with sparks of genius.

Challenges are no big deal to me, because I approach them with confidence and ease. I align myself with peace and calm. I am centered. I am relaxed. From this space, answers float to me like wisps on a breeze.

I am grateful. I am worthy. I am generous. I am love. Thank you, life.

I'm my own gorgeous hero. I am having my moment now, the power is building in my bones. The answers are all around me. So easy to see. Yes! Yes! Yes! It's all within me.

I am lifted up by so much love for myself, I'm brilliant, and I feel like I can reach out and touch the sky. Peppermint pink clouds surround me, soft, supportive, and I feel so amazingly high.

I dazzle with problem-solving prowess. It suffuses me. I am magnificent.

I am success. I am in the right place, at the right time, solving and winning the best challenges.

I choose to live the most incredible life. A life full of artistry, vision, individuality, and expressiveness.

I transcend, I radiate love, I'm a believer. I wake up every morning with warmth and courage in my heart. Compassion and growth tickling me. I believe. I believe. I believe... in the power of ME.

Ideas and solutions zigzag around me and through me. I have the answers.

Oddball solutions are my specialty. Kooky. Bizarre. Creative. Brilliant. These all come naturally to me.

I am a perfect vibrational match for my desired, creative outcome. I approach problems with the ease of leisure.

I keep going. Always and forever. I am a victor! ROAARRR!

Brainstorming badass solutions is a cakewalk!

Ideas are infinite. Answers are infinite. My creativity is infinite!

I am a Problem-Solving Ninja. I sneak up on problems, and answers rush to me from all sides.

When a problem arises, my face lights up! It's time for fun, and I have a big ol' smile. I am ready. I embrace it. Let's do this!

I believe in the highest expression of me. My spirit soars, bursting out of me, flying to places unknown.

Kindness and compassion fill my heart with peace, and this allows me to persevere at all times.

I keep my heart uplifted in spite of any circumstances. This is true greatness.

I slide through problems like a sly, sexy fox, having fun solving them thinking outside the box.

My creative genius makes fantastic opportunities out of all kinds of problems. They are a source of inspiration for me!

Creativity Tip: Ask Better Questions

Personal development guru Tony Robbins says we can improve our lives if we *ask better questions*. It's true, because the brain is actually quite good at generating answers to questions. You'd think that the smartest people are the ones who are best at coming up with answers. But the smartest people are actually those who ask the best questions.

Here's an easy example we can all relate to. Suppose there's something you need to do that you're not excited about, like cleaning the garage. Let's assume the garage is a disaster, and you don't even know where to start.

You could ask yourself,

How should I go about cleaning the garage?

Or, you could ask a better version of the question:

How could I clean the garage and have fun in the process?

Or,

How could I clean the garage and get exercise at the same time?

See how just asking a different question focuses your brain on a completely different solution?

Perhaps the answer to both of these is to play music and dance while doing the cleaning. Either way, this technique helps you see possibilities that you might not have otherwise noticed, by changing where your brain looks for answers.

CHAPTER 9

WINE SELF-TALK SCRIPT: PERMISSION TO GO FULL WOO-WOO

> *Science means constantly walking a tightrope between blind faith and curiosity; between expertise and creativity; between bias and openness; between experience and epiphany; between ambition and passion; and between arrogance and conviction. In short, between an old today and a new tomorrow.*
>
> — Heinrich Rohrer

I sit here dictating this chapter you're reading right now, in my *Juju Corner.*

It's a corner in my mom's house in Arizona where we're visiting. The definition of juju: *supernatural power attributed to a charm.* Or in my case, a corner of the room. Yup, that's sounds about right. In my Juju Corner, I'm staring at all the quartz crystals I have placed around me. I love the shapes. I love their density and hardness; it reminds me of strength. I love the colors, and gazing upon this kind of natural art *elevates my emotions.*

I often think about the claims some people make about the "energy" of these crystals. People who get labeled as "woo-woo." Do I believe in it? Can this amethyst or smoky quartz actually heal? Do they attract wealth? I have no idea. But there is one thing of which I am sure. They change the energy in this little corner, because they inspire *me to change my energy*. When I see them, they elevate my emotions. And that's a great thing! Elevated thoughts and feelings draw my incredible dreams to me faster.

So, yeah, call me *Woo-Woo Woman*. I dig it.

With that in mind, I encourage all of you to get a little *woo*. If you already are, then good for you. You'll love this script. But I'm actually even more excited about the people who are *not* woo, and who embrace this lesson with an open mind... at least, using woo to enhance your creativity. Because we all know the creative process is a little *mysterious* anyway, right? I mean, the whole creativity thing is pretty damn woo, if you think about it. It can be profound for the practical thinkers out there. If Einstein can come up with the Theory of Relativity while dreaming on a train, that's good enough proof for me. Woo opens your mind, giving you permission to shut down the analytical part of your brain and go waaaay *out there* with your pondering. Like Pablo Picasso said, "*The chief enemy of creativity is 'good sense.'*"

The script at the end of this chapter is designed to give you *Permission to Go Full Woo-Woo*, to inspire buckets of *creativity and novelty* in your life. Permission to fully explore "*What If?*" questions on a glittering magic carpet ride. I recommend doing this in a few different ways, to seek ideas and questions by journeying on one of the following paths for inspiration (or something similar of your own imagination):

- Creativity Talisman & Special Effects
- Nature and Her Massive Powers
- Geeking Out in Speculative Fiction Land
- Future Goggles
- Ol' Timey Time Travel

You may not spend a lot of time contemplating such things, or perhaps you only do when you're reading a novel, or watching an insanely awesome show like *The Expanse*. But these are super opportunities to expand your mind. To instill some *otherworldly and creative* thoughts, so they can ooze around your brain and get absorbed into your *practical, everyday* thoughts. That's when crazy-awesome ideas are born. It's when the mundane ideas make sweet love to the weird ideas that something amazing pops out, and we give birth to something truly innovative.

As a novelist, I find this kind of thinking to be invaluable for my writing. But more importantly, it's a general-purpose method for solving problems, with staggering benefits. Watching sci-fi won't make you suddenly invent warp drive technology, but when you habitually consider things that do not yet exist, your brain fires and wires as it gets into the *habit* of coming up with new ideas of any kind. Such as things to help with everyday life. Fire and wire that creative process, my friend.

Let's go on a magic carpet ride of woo!

Creativity Talisman & Special Effects

First, get yourself a *creativity talisman*... maybe some crystals or fairy figurines. Or a stuffed unicorn plush toy, or some Star Wars action figures. Sparkly things, a book on mythical creatures, or a pewter wine goblet embossed with a heraldic dragon. Or perhaps create a special mood effect, such as with candles, a red lava lamp, incense, or one of those groovy lights that projects stars onto the ceiling... whatever you want. If you have an object, place it on your desk or nightstand. Or hold it while you read your *Permission to Go Full Woo-Woo* Wine Self-Talk Script.

Nature & Her Massive Powers

When I sit and really think about nature, I am spectacularly awed by her powers. They seem so magical. Subtle at times, gargantuan at others. Babies being born, and flowers, growing from seeds into all kinds of shapes and colors. Bumblebees and hummingbirds and caterpillars. The tides and the full moon. The very bottom, deepest depths of the sea, where insane, freaky-ass creatures lurk... I mean, *glow-in-the-dark* stuff... and *giant squids*? *Wtf?* Chills go down my spine —that's what I feel when I think about nature. And this, it's all incredible fodder for the creative soul.

Take some time and think about nature and her elements that give you the biggest goosebumps. Do a search online and look for images of nature that make your jaw drop. Make it a habit. It's a great way to invoke more creativity into your life, because it allows you to witness things that exist at an almost incomprehensibly grand scale.

Geeking Out in Speculative Fiction Land

I also use *speculative fiction* and movies about outer space as an opportunity to detach my thinking from ordinary, day-to-day things. *To see farther*, if you will. To think about possibilities, with no constraints. I let myself get drawn into these crazy ideas, which always lead me into a *holy shit, what if?* mindset. What if we could really incubate babies in artificial wombs? What would that do to society? Or, what if people could live forever? What would that mean? Or, if we could colonize Mars in ten years, would I go? What would it be like?

The more you let your mind entertain these fantastic terrains, the easier it becomes to imagine things that haven't happened yet.

When I was growing up, my thoughts about science fiction were very simplistic. In fact, my only real exposure was *Star Wars,* which I only watched because my older brother was into it. I liked Chewbacca and Princess Leia.

When I met Greg, he introduced me to science fiction at a deeper level… turns out *Star Wars* is technically more like fantasy set in space, whereas more literary speculative fiction (which includes science-fiction) contemplates some really deep shit. Like what it really means to be human. And what comprises humanity's potential. And what things might be like in the future. The more movies and TV shows I watched, and the more books I read, the more ways my mind learned to bend and twist. So when I added these ideas and themes to my *Permission to Go Full Woo-Woo*, my mind blew up with thoughts and questions. Now, just sitting in my living room, I can embrace a speculative mindset and let my mind wander in all different ways, even as I think about practical issues in the real world, such as what could happen in the *near* future with technology, social media, democracy, demographic trends, or certain stocks.

Future Goggles

My husband has a knack for spotting trends early. He built his first e-commerce website in 1995, when so-called "experts" on CNN were literally saying "the Internet is just a fad," and "nobody will ever buy anything from a stranger on the computer." He was an investor in one of the first 3D printer companies. He bought Tesla in 2013 at $28 a share. And Bitcoin when it was $300 (as of this writing, it's $50,000). I've learned to take his crazy predictions seriously. In fact, he says,

If it doesn't sound a little crazy, you're already too late.

Years ago, when ebooks were brand new, and Greg and I were first launching my blog and recipe book publishing business, we had some aggressive timelines, which often made it feel like a frivolous distraction to spend time reading about things that didn't relate directly to the business. But I was reminded of a quote I'd once read:

Leaders don't have time to read, but people who don't read aren't fit for leadership.

In other words, whether you've got time or not, you have to keep feeding your brain new information (whether it's reading, or other formats, like podcasts, etc.).

So we officially gave ourselves permission to spend time at this, even when the benefits were not immediately obvious. You never know what's going to end up being important. Some of it pays off later, some of it doesn't.

We came up with a code word for the idea of exploring all kinds of things that might end up being important one day: *Future Goggles.*

The code word served as a reminder, not only to always keep exploring new things, but also to always deliberately keep our minds open to looking for trends. So, for instance, I might email a link to Greg, with *Future Goggles* in the subject line, so that he knows why I'm sending him the link, the implication being that it might relate to some trend he's interested in watching.

This might seem like a weird code word for a couple to have, but from the moment we said it, it had a profound effect. In that moment, it was like we strapped on some high-tech goggles, and we could suddenly see more *futury* things and opportunities. In reality, we were just formalizing the idea to be on the lookout for interesting stuff. Like it was an official part of our jobs. When you direct your brain to "look for something blue," you start to notice blue things. Well, same goes for telling your brain to look for potential opportunities.

The opportunities could be anything... ideas of things to invent based on thinking about a future need of society. It could be a stock to invest in based on some trend. It could be about taking sensible precautions in case of a natural disaster or economic downturn.

What a great way to use creativity, right? It's so fun! We always have the most interesting conversations, speculating about the possible implications of some piece of news. Especially the non-obvious things, which is where the biggest opportunities are. We'd look at our current life and then imagine what could happen in the near future, and strategize about how to capitalize on it. And how to solve or avoid any potential problems we saw coming on the horizon.

Looking for trends became our habit, so when something popped up online or in the news, my mind would automatically go to making connections. Ideas would spark, and they continue doing so to this day, almost fifteen years later!

Even when the ideas don't result in anything that we act upon, the exercise itself is invaluable for enhancing our creative processes and problem-solving skills. As an aside, it's been wonderful for our relationship, too... always discussing the future together, whether it's our own future or the whole world's.

Ol' Timey Time Travel

Inspired by Diana Gabaldon's famous novels and TV-series, *Outlander*, I couldn't help but regularly wonder, *every time* I watched the show, how being from the future and traveling back in time, you would have such clarity about many aspects of the future, and the changes that would be coming. Maybe it's just me, but the idea of knowing the future, and comparing it to the older way of life, really changed how I viewed the world and boosted my creative thinking.

When I wasn't watching the show, I'd find myself mentally time traveling back to *ol' timey* times. I'd picture life in the past, such as the 1700s, or the Old West, and imagine what it must have been like, and how they did things. I'd look around and ask myself, what big things are missing? Like antibiotics. Or air-conditioning. Or cotton swabs! Hehe. What was needed to make these changes? What stood in the way of progress? And then, in this weird, altered frame of mind, I looked around at my current, present-day life, trying to imagine what amazing things await us *in our own future*, and what stands in the way of *that* progress. And once again, I find my creative thinking bursting at the seams. Not with 100% useful ideas, but rather, with *so many* ideas, that the best 2% are real keepers. With creativity, quality comes from *quantity* of ideas.

~

It's all about exercising the creative muscle, and when you access your creativity with *woo*, you give yourself permission to think *waaaay* outside the box, whether it's magic, time travel, or whatever you want. Use everything and anything to pump up your imagination, like you're pumping up a bouncy house. You'll be bowled over at the connections and freshness that come into your life when you flood your thoughts with this type of meandering and mind-expanding exercises.

So give yourself permission to go full woo-woo, whether that's believing in angels, or aliens, or pretending that the summertime fireflies at dusk are actually little woodland fairies. (Psst... *they are.*) Whether that means placing a citrine crystal next to your laptop to inspire financial success, or an amethyst geode under your pillow to inspire relaxation and dreams... *and* rose quartz crystals in the corners of your bedroom, to inspire some sweet-n-saucy love... it all inspires creativity as you fire and wire up your powerful imagination to unleash your *inner genius*.

Permission to woo is really permission to use your imagination and take it as far as you can. After all, it was one of my heroes, Albert Einstein, who said,

Imagination is more important than knowledge. Knowledge is limited. Imagination encircles the world.

Wine Self-Talk Script: Permission to Go Full Woo-Woo

I love thinking creatively, and I am open to all ideas, in all ways.

I am so in-tune with myself with confidence and comfy love, I'm ready and open for blazing, fiery, new ideas! Magic carpet ride, here I come.

I am expanded with knowing. I am empowered with imagination. I am a creator.

I will always show my ideas, I will always show how I really feel, because my feelings and ideas are valid and valued.

I have a beautiful heart, full of gratitude and love for all of my blessings.

I don my high-tech, Future Goggles, and I speculate about all kinds of exciting things.

I am coming alive. I am open wide and electrified, with star-filled love for myself, for my life, for my inspirations shooting around me like comets in the sky.

I am worthy of creativity and brilliant ideas.

I am grateful for my newness and vision.

I appreciate my originality, my newfound love of the unknown, and the magic rumbling in my bones.

I am in awe of nature and her miracles. They awaken my own creative powers.

I have a job, one job: to love myself. We all deserve to love ourselves so we can light up the world for others.

I choose people for my life who see me, let me be me, who want me to win. I do the same for them.

I love tapping into my intuition for enlightening guidance. I close my eyes, take a luxurious breath, and feel my way to the answers.

From time travel, to rocket ships made of gold, I think about it all. My mind wanders free, to the edges of the galaxy. I delight, because I am drawn to this creativity.

Anything is possible. I open my eyes to the sky. I fill my heart with love, and I'm on my way to creative play.

My imagination dances with stars, fairies, and gnomes. My ideas connect and spark inside me. I am so very much alive!

The tiniest, unexpected change could shift my entire life onto a completely new trajectory. I am open to all possibilities.

I am supported by the magical energy of the universe. I am distinctive. I am ready. I am here to live and play at the highest level.

Creativity responds to my thoughts and feelings. I am skilled and imaginative. New ideas connect inside me all hours of the day and night.

Creativity Tip: Creativity Born from Meditation

Research shows that certain types of meditation can assist creative thinking. You may have thought of meditation as just a way to relax and reduce stress, but the benefits go much further.

Plop your butt down in a comfy spot, close your eyes, and go on an *ommmm* magic yoga mat ride. To boost the creative process while meditating, make sure you keep an open focus, so really let your mind go black and blank. Being receptive to any and all. No tight focus on any single thing. Let random thoughts and ideas float through the blank, black canvas of your mind, and simply observe them. Set a timer for two minutes, and reminders to do this a few times a week.

CHAPTER 10

WINE SELF-TALK SCRIPT: CREATIVE CONFIDENCE

> *Life should not be a journey to the grave with the intention of arriving safely in a pretty and well-preserved body, but rather, to skid in broadside in a cloud of smoke, thoroughly used up, totally worn out, and loudly proclaiming "Wow! What a ride!"*
>
> — Hunter S. Thompson

I love that quote. I remind myself of it whenever I feel like I'm living with too many rules. A life noosed by restrictions. I pull out the quote, read it a few times, and then go off to live life with fewer rules and more confidence. More risks, more rewards. And more fun.

Living with too many rules is living with the guardrails on. Guardrails are great for bowling when you're five years old, but at some point, you need to remove them.

Besides, there's much more opportunity for success when you let yourself go wild... running, jumping, and playing. This is especially true with creativity. It's coloring outside the lines, making new art along the way, and boldly skipping into new opportunities every day.

When I had my first idea for a romance novel, I wondered if it was a sign that I should travel down a new road... becoming a novelist. I had a moment where I thought, "Sure, I have an idea for a story. But is that it? Just one?"

Turns out, no.

I used my self-talk to my advantage, and I chose to imagine my life writing *many* novels, confident that, if I could come up with one idea, then I could come up with lots of them. I chose to believe in *abundance*. I repeatedly told myself, *I'm a creative genius,* over and over. I even had that line engraved on my Apple AirPods case! When I regularly reminded myself that I am, indeed, a creative genius, I squashed any mental barriers, such as:

But I don't have a degree in creative writing.

But I've never written even a short story.

What do I know about writing fiction?

It's safer to keep writing nonfiction and blogging.

But. But. But.

Guardrails. Rules. Nooses.

And with those thoughts vetoed, overridden, and overthrown, my mind opened up to possibilities. I crashed through my doubts and stifling rules. I chose to be confident in my ability to create. With no rules, just inspired passion. Most of all, I chose to believe that my creative well would always be full of ideas.

At first, I had no reason to think this way. I had never done anything like this in my life. But I knew about the power of the brain, and my intuition was telling me *I could do anything*. As always, it started with my mindset, and my self-talk:

I'm a creative genius.

I'm a creative genius.

I am an amazing, brilliant, creative genius!

I kept repeating these words, over and over and over. Not just every morning during my Coffee Self-Talk, but throughout the day as well.

And you know what? I started to believe it.

A few days later, I woke up one morning feeling like I'd swallowed a *creative genius* pill, and it was just matter-of-fact that the pill had done its job. I walked through my house confident that, *of course*, it'll happen.

The more I told myself, *I'm a creative genius*, the more confident I became about my creativity, even before writing the first word of a novel. It was like a dimmer switch inside me was slowly turning up my confidence... this crazy belief that I could do it. Can you imagine how weird it would be to never have done something, but to feel like you already somehow knew how to do it? As if I had been an author in a past life, and I had this author DNA inside me, and it had just now been switched on!

That's what my self-talk does to me. It might feel foreign the first few times I say something new, but it soon starts to feel intrinsic, like it's a part of me. A knowing, deep down in my bones. And this knowing creates the most amazing feelings—amazing *confidence*—and *THAT* makes manifesting happen.

Only a few nights later, as I was trying to fall asleep, my mind started to explode with story ideas. In one of them, heroine and hero come together in an *opposites-attract* story. In another, it was a classic friends-to-lovers scenario. In another, it was a... wait for it... *sports romance* story. Sports romance? Whaaa? Where are these ideas coming from?

I was overwhelmed. Not only with all of the story lines rushing to me all at once, but dumbfounded that it was even happening. To me. I yanked my phone off the nightstand, fumbling in the dark, and started frantically tapping all of the ideas into my Evernote app, one after the other. I still feel tingly when I think about it. To this day, it still feels so damned magical.

Those Crucial Next Steps

When an idea comes to you, there's the whole notion of *What do I do about it?*

Do I totally shift gears in my life and head in a whole new direction? I wondered if writing the novel would be a colossal waste of time. What if nothing came of it? *Blah Blah blah...* I mean, *stop!* How could exploring creativity *ever* be a waste of time? You can't fail. Even if I never sold a single copy of my book, I knew that at some level, the process of writing it would improve my life. All else being equal, creative lives are *more fun.*

Creative lives are more fun because they're more colorful, naturally invigorating, and interesting. After I started writing fiction, I started to see the world differently. I became more aware of my surroundings. I saw buildings in new light and shadows. I noticed how the trees move in the breeze, and I thought about how I would describe them in written words. I started paying close attention to nature and human behavior. I considered it all research for my writing, but it became such an amazing way to live, because I was so much more *present* with every step I took.

It also enriched my life in other ways, like solving problems. The nature of doing something artistic cracked my mind wide open to new things. I'm now always on the lookout for new ideas, new connections, and new answers to old questions.

All of this increased my confidence.

Of course, traveling off the beaten path can also create uncertainty in life. But as Shekhar Kapur said,

> *I have devoted my life to uncertainty. Certainty is the death of wisdom, thought, creativity.*

If I wanted to live a more distinctive life, with fresh air blowing through my days, then I'd want more creativity. If the price of that is some uncertainty, then it's a price I'm willing to pay. Uncertainty can even be *exciting!*

Uncertainty need not erode your confidence. In fact, once you get used to living with uncertainty, just the opposite happens. You learn to trust that you'll be fine no matter what the future brings.

One way to develop confidence about your creativity is to make sure that creativity and inventiveness are always welcome in your mind. Tell yourself to *expect* creativity. Open your life to it. Find some creative things to do to encourage it. Make the conditions in your mind ripe for creative exploration, with no expectations. Like a farmer tilling the soil, these attitudes make the conditions perfect for planting seeds so the seeds bear fruit.

The same thing happens for your ideas and creativity. You want the best conditions to plant seeds, and Wine Self-Talk offers this. Along with all the ideas sprinkled throughout in this book. The more you do it, the more your creativity expands, and this gives you greater confidence that your creativity will continue to flow.

Keep on Moving

You always want to keep your momentum going. Keep moving. Forever onward. What do I mean by this? When you come up with an idea, you can decide whether to do something about it or not. If not, file it away for possible future use. If you do decide to go forward with the idea and push something out there into the world, that's great! But then... you keep on moving. Detached from the outcome.

Come again?

Put my heart and soul into something and then detach from it? My *baby*?

Yup.

You always want to keep the energy of creativity flowing *forward*. It's easy to become attached to our creative endeavors, and that's fine when you're in the middle of a project, but once you're done, and you put it out into the world, people will respond to it however they will, with praise or criticism. Or more likely, both. Don't let your ego get involved. It only creates unnecessary stress. If you get too attached to your creations, it can put you in an emotional survival state. Fear, anxiety, worry, and self-doubt. To hell with those! You don't need 'em.

Instead, just put your creative efforts out into the world, with love, and don't look back. Move on. Next project!

This kind of clearheaded detachment fuels a calm demeanor and increases your confidence as you progress from one project to the next, confident, always knowing there's something new on the horizon. So much great stuff still to do!

Detachment doesn't mean you can't visualize great success! You absolutely can, for any project, or for your creative efforts in general. But don't get caught up *depending* on success to make you happy, or you'll become a prisoner to people's opinions, reviews, sales, likes, retweets, etc. It's much better to be free-flowing. Relaxed. In this healthy frame of mind, you'll be more detached after a project launches, which makes it that much easier to start your next project.

Emotional detachment offers you a secret edge, an advantage in everything you do. It allows you to diversify. To experiment, without fear. It allows you to keep creating and keep putting new things out there. Some will do better than others. That's normal. Don't give it much thought. *Just keep on going!*

Wine Self-Talk Script: Creative Confidence

I love confidence, and confidence loves me. I am worthy.

I have so many original ideas. They're hanging off trees, ripe and ready for me to pick.

My life is strong. I am confident and creative. I take chances because I can.

I've got my hand on the throttle, ready to drive into my best life ever!

I'm jazzed for my clever new life! Tip! Tap! Swish!

I relax my mind. I see creativity opportunities everywhere I look.

Ideas collide and intersect, breeding new creations in my mind.

Confidence. Bravery. Courage. All in my back pocket. They're me. They're mine. I go-go-go, fueled by these amazing truths.

My expectations and standards are perfect. I am incredibly confident, and I shine.

I love taking chances, and I bet on my creativity every day of the year.

I regularly check in with my desires, for every choice I make. I ask myself, "Am I enjoying this? Does it make me come alive? Does it stir my soul?" This reminds me to stay true to myself and have fun.

I am confident!

I win, you win, everyone wins with self-love.

I'm worthy of the most crazy, fun, and rambunctious life, filled with cheer, treasure, and love. Rah! Rah! Rah!

I attract an overflow of creativity into my life. Synchronicities are around every corner. Money, Magic, Creative Confidence, and Magnificence. All here for me.

I am grateful for my life and for my creativity. It's always here.

I love my creative life. I love life. I love my ingenuity and creative genius.

Life is a gift, a rainbow of colors. I appreciate it all. Thank you, life. Thank you, me.

I pass a mirror and see my smiling reflection. I say, "Hi, hot stuff! You're creative!"

I'm THE NEW ME! I love my new creative self. I rise every day with shine, I glide through time on a breeze with ease, I fall asleep with peace.

I am resourceful, and this fuels my confidence. I am resourceful, and I know what I want. I am resourceful, I can do it. I am resourceful, I AM doing it!

All is well. We are all one. When we connect our souls and hearts from all different cultures, innovation explodes.

I am confident in my goals, dreams, and desires. I know that my creativity brings me closer to them every day. With confidence, I am expressive, and drawing my magnificent dreams faster to me.

Creativity Tip: Creating Creative Conditions

One way to make creativity more accessible, aside from your Wine Self-Talk, is to simply make room for it in your life. Think about that... *making room for creativity*.

Yes, creativity needs *space*.

It needs space to stretch out and reach into different parts of your brain, *your life*, to make novel connections you hadn't considered before. It needs space in your mind and attention. It needs space in your daily planner.

Let's take a moment and look at your life to see what takes up space in your mind. What preoccupies you routinely, possibly even nagging you? Do you have a constant to-do list running inside the hamster wheel of your mind? Do you find yourself getting frequently annoyed, feeling prickly, like you just ran through a field of stinging nettle?

Sometimes, little things eat away at us throughout the day, like a caterpillar munching through a leaf. Or annoyances that create tension, and we don't even realize we're expending energy on them, because they're in the background. Like the noisy hum of a fan that you only notice, with relief, when it gets turned off. The problem is that people tolerate that noise. Too much, for too long. We think it's "just life."

Well, no. It's not. It doesn't have to be that way.

Look at your schedule for the next week, and carve out some time for creativity in your life. Create the conditions for creativity to feel welcome, and then watch what amazing things happen!

CHAPTER 11

WINE SELF-TALK SCRIPT: HAPPY HAMMOCK HOUR

During rest, about 750 milliliters of blood—enough to fill a full wine bottle —flows through the brain every minute.

— *James Nestor, Breath*

You're chilling out in a hammock. Resting. Your feet are kicked up, you're gazing at your sexy toes. Deep and easy breaths. Refreshing coconut water in hand. Sun shining overhead. *Ahhh!* It sounds so good.

That day will come, right? Someday. Because who has time to take a rest or vacation right now? Let alone *scheduling rest* as a regular part of your... wait for it... *every day?*

I mean, really. Who does that?

Well, it turns out... some of the smartest, most creative, most talented, and most productive people in the world do. They rest with the same level of intention as they work. They even schedule rests and naps on their calendar app!

Most of us think that rest is for *after* a full day of work. Or after a hard week. Or after decades of working, in retirement. You know, after you've *earned* it.

That's how I always viewed rest. But I couldn't have been more wrong. What I didn't know for so long—like, 30 years—was about the incredible magic of *rest*. The simple act of taking a bit of time away from work makes you more productive when you get back to work than if you hadn't taken a break. Imagine... taking breaks boosts *overall* productivity. How I wish I'd known this 30 years ago... things would have been SO much better!

My Life "Before" Rest

Not too long ago, I was one of those people who worked 16-hour days. Not all on my computer; I might've been writing for 6 to 8 hours, but the other 8-10 hours, I was constantly thinking about what to write next. So in a way, I was still working the whole time. Never a break. When I went swimming, I'd think about work, and stories, and author stuff. When I was cooking, I was thinking about work. When I was peeing or showering, I was thinking about work.

Sounds a little unbalanced, right?

I felt guilty whenever I rested. For every minute I wasn't actively thinking or working on a project, or a book, or marketing, I felt like I wasn't moving forward. Or worse... like I was backsliding.

But then one day, something tugged inside me that said, *This is not the way to live.* This is not the way to manifest abundance. I began to realize I was on a dangerous road to *Burn-Out Town*.

But what I didn't know was that my intuition had a lot of solid science behind it.

That's right, the science of *resting*! Studies have shown that taking your mind off of work makes you *more* productive. It even makes you more successful in your career! It turns out that rest and work are partners. In fact, many of history's most brilliant minds in science, art, and mathematics, had humongous insights during the times they were resting and *skillfully* pursuing leisure.

Rest for Creativity

It turns out that rest is a critical ingredient for boosting your creativity. When you rest, you are more relaxed. When you're more relaxed, you're less stressed. Stress disconnects you from life, from solutions, from opportunities. Stress even makes you forget to breathe properly. You know, nice, long, deep breaths.

Stress makes you focus on the minutia, which impairs your ability to connect the dots, to see the big picture. Author Natalie Goldberg applies this idea to time, saying that being stressed is living with life,

> *...diced up into minutes and hours rather than into seasons and the movement of the moon and sun.*

What a gorgeous way to see living and time. Imagine how much less stressful you'd be if you focused on seasons and lunar cycles instead of hours and minutes.

Natalie writes how-to books for writers, but her advice is good for everyone, and one of my favorites is that she "gives you permission to be *lazy*."

I'm talkin' *full-on* lazy, like just-lie-down lazy, and do absolutely nothing. It's actually not a waste of time. When you're doing "nothing," your subconscious goes to work. You're not aware of it... that's why it's subconscious. Things start to percolate beneath the surface. Eventually, the percolating subconscious thoughts settle, and things just magically become clear to you. This clarity makes everything easier. You make better decisions. You're more confident about what to do next. It allows you to make more interesting connections, to come up with more creative solutions, and to experience more flourishing creativity in general.

In short, having clarity makes you *smarter.*

Which is to say, *resting* makes you smarter.

> *The mind is like water. When it's turbulent, it's difficult to see. When it's calm, everything becomes clear.*
>
> — Prasad Mahes

Resting calms the soul. For years, I thought rest was what you do on vacation. The very picture is wired into my brain: A beach. A margarita. Lounging lazily in a hammock in the shade of a coconut palm tree.

Now, I don't live on the beach, but this mental image provides a kind of target. I know how proper rest is supposed to *feel.* It's supposed to feel like a little *vacation* in the middle of my day. Therefore, when I say I'm going to "rest" come 1:00 p.m.—every day—I turn on the wave machine for some island sound effects, and I lay down and close my eyes for twenty minutes. Margarita optional! (Haha, just kidding... that would knock me out for the rest of the day.)

This little change to my daily work routine has had a profound effect on my life. When I get up from my tropical mini-vacay, I'm all energized and rarin' to go!

I know, sounds decadent, right?

Remember, the science backs it up. It doesn't just *feel* good, it *is* good! During leisure time, the brain secretes dopamine, that exquisite, neurotransmitter that gushes good feelings all through us. That's why resting feels good. But the reason it actually works is because the downtime also increases activity in different parts of your brain... which causes those connections between disparate parts, thereby spiking your creativity. It's like making money while you sleep—literally and figuratively! Your mind *on rest* shifts into lighting up the *default mode network*. This is the area of the brain for imagination, dreaming, and introspection, and it's super important for creativity and problem solving.

The Rest "Respawning" Effect

Stepping away from work for a brief rest almost feels like it resets you. Like a character in a video game who respawns with 100% health. This means improved vigor and more energy! Which not only allows you to be more creative, it makes you better at *all work*... even the kind that doesn't require creative thinking.

The Swaggering Superhero

Getting rest is a clever hack for increasing your confidence. Your *swagger*.

How? Well, by scheduling rest into your every day, you start to feel a tremendous new source of power. It means you're taking control of your schedule. You're *in charge*. It's lack of control that makes us feel the highest levels of tension and stress. Or worse, depression. But when you get the edge in life, taking control of your schedule and doing something as audacious as *taking a nap* (or whatever you do to unwind... shoot some hoops, work a jigsaw puzzle, etc.), it's going to give you the swagger of a super-confident *superhero*.

Naps: My Favorite Way to Rest

When I started taking daily naps, it changed my creativity and my life.

Sleep is so important, for sanity, health, and magical living, that I wrote a book about it, *Pillow Self-Talk*. Sleep is also paramount for its role in your creative thinking and processing of information. I'm now making the craziest connections as I'm falling asleep, or when I first wake up. It's actually pretty spooky how regularly it happens now, almost like I'm channeling some kind of sacred knowledge from the ethers while I'm asleep, plugged into the Magic of the Universe. (Pro-tip: Keep a notebook or your phone handy to jot down notes upon waking, right away, before you forget.)

Some very smart people have known the value of taking naps. People like Aristotle, Thomas Edison, Margaret Thatcher, and Winston Churchill. Winston really took his naps seriously. He said,

> *You must sleep sometime between lunch and dinner, and no half-way measures. Take off your clothes, and get into bed. Don't think you will be doing less work because you sleep during the day. That's a foolish notion held by people who have no imagination. You will be able to accomplish more. You get two days in one—well, at least one and a half, I'm sure. When the war started, I had to sleep during the day because that was the only way I could cope with my responsibilities.*

Thomas Edison would analyze the details of a problem and then lie down to rest. "Within minutes," he said, "the solution would flash to me out of the air."

When I learned about all of this enchanting rest stuff, I was inspired to take it seriously. I mean, if famous scientists, and tech giants, and artists the world over, from time immemorial, aren't chained to their desks, why should I be?

The Rainbow Colors of Rest: So Many Choices!

But sleep isn't the only form of the reinvigorating rest that's available to you. Rest also comes in the form of passive leisure activities, walking, spending time in nature, doing hobbies, vigorous exercise, and other intense forms of "play." You might not think of rest and exercise as being one in the same, but to your brain, they are. If you enjoy the exercise, and if it's intense enough, you enter *flow*, getting into *the zone*

—and then it *is* considered rest for your brain, which enhances creativity.

Making rest a super skill of yours is a smart move. It's strategic. And when you look at it in this light, you approach resting with intention, which is really to say that you take it seriously. And planning it means knowing in advance the different options you have for resting, so you can put it on your daily calendar.

The Ultimate Rest: Vacations

> *One in five startup ideas come to entrepreneurs while on vacation.*
>
> — *Forbes.com*

The point of resting is to give your mind a break from actively and consciously working on your work or trying to solve your problems. Whether the break means a stroll through a park, or playing the piano, or cooking an omelette, or playing with LEGO, strategically taking your mind off work does legit wonders for you.

And then there's the ultimate mental break: You can take a vacation.

You might be tempted to laugh at this one, thinking, well, obviously vacations are for rest. But the crazy thing is that so many people take their problems—and their work—with them on vacation. That is not a smart use of their vacation. It's not actual rest if the brain doesn't stop doing what it normally does at work.

Vacations are the ultimate pattern interrupt. Vacations change your location, surroundings, schedule, activities, and of course, thoughts. At times like this, when you step away from everything that is familiar, your creative insights can explode. Which explains the quote from Forbes.com above, "*One in five startup ideas come to entrepreneurs while on vacation.*"

That's a staggering statistic. Even if you're not into starting companies, it kind of makes you want to take a vacation—right now—just to see what awesome ideas you might come up with!

> *There is virtue in work, and there is virtue in rest.*
>
> — Alan Cohen

Let's dive into a script that encourages more rest to help you live your most creative and happy life.

Wine Self-Talk Script: Happy Hammock Hour

Rest is a smart tool, and I strategically use rest to improve my creativity.

I care for myself first so that I, too, can care for others properly. Vacations, naps, and playtime are perfect.

I love the power I feel in my soul to design my magical life. I hold the master key to my kingdom of self-love, and the creative genius to accomplish anything I desire.

I love a good, solid nap, because I wake up from it refreshed and bright-eyed.

I have a skip in my step and music in my soul. I am worthy of every dream I have. I love me.

I recharge my own golden light so I can shine bright for myself and for others.

I keep my heart and mind uplifted. This is greatness.

After taking time to play and have fun, my eyes are focused, my soul is on fire. I am ready to do it all.

I use resting, naps, and delicious sleep to amp up my creativity. It works every time!

I am a brand-new, sparkling, brilliant person. I look into my luminous eyes, and I see a universe of possibility looking back, reflecting pure self-love.

I am rested! I am filled with peace! I am creative!

Nourishing my soul with acts of self-care, makes me feel wonderful and content, like I'm floating on air.

I say no when I want to say no, and I say yes when I want to say yes. That's a powerful act of self-love.

I am calm. My heart is full of peace, and I breathe beautiful, relaxed breaths.

I elevate myself, my ideas, and my magnificence when I take time for me.

I am worthy of resting. You are worthy of resting. We are all worthy of resting.

I am happy. I eagerly enjoy my happy hammock time, where I unwind, uncoil, and my creative juices simmer in my mind.

I am in tune with my magical self, alive with creative awareness, and I tap into my inner genius at a moment's notice.

Self-love flows to me in abundance. I am rich in rest. I am wealthy in self-worth and self-care. I attract a joyful, creative life, full of riches, innovation, and love.

Acts of self-love are my norm, my jammy jam, my specialty. I kick back with easy confidence all the time.

I believe in me, because I can do whatever I put my incredible mind to. Cleverness and epic living are here.

Sizzle. Lightning. Thunder. Ideas are stewing and brewing inside me, all the time.

I love taking time for myself. I know with all my heart that proper rest and a mind that's still, and full of peace, are the ultimate recipe for my creativity.

I respect the seasons of living, and the waves of day to day. I honor my visions and plant seeds of gifted ingenuity. I nourish and water them with rest and playful meandering. And then I harvest the huge rewards.

Yes. Yes! Rest is the best.

Creativity Tip: Schedule Your Rest!

Even though working nonstop can give you a false sense of productivity (been there, done that), it can also rob you of energy in the long run. And snuff out your creative spark!

So, if you're the type of person who thrives on intensity, make it a point to take scheduled breaks. I have it in my calendar to take a nap a few times a week. I also have it in my calendar to play UNO with my daughter every three nights.

Sometimes you have to schedule rest in your calendar to remind yourself to do it. There's nothing wrong with that; it's too easy to forget otherwise. Over time, your *rest date* will become a standing appointment, and you will come to expect this special time, and love what it does for you and your creativity.

CHAPTER 12

WINE SELF-TALK SCRIPT: FALLING IN LOVE WITH YOUR JUICY INTUITION

> *Sometimes you've got to let everything go—purge yourself. If you are unhappy with anything... whatever is bringing you down, get rid of it. Because you'll find that when you're free, your true creativity, your true self comes out.*
>
> — TINA TURNER

Becoming more intimate with your intuition is a spectacular way to improve your creativity. But how do you do that? It's easy. You start with your mind. You want to get *very close* to it.

Imagine having a romantic date with your subconscious. An imaginary candle-lit dinner, just you and your juicy intuition. Soft music playing in the background. Red wine. You share a chocolate lava cake.

You want to *fall in love* with your juicy intuition!

And trust it.

And you tap into it for creativity.

So, first things first. Invite your intuition to play by asking it out on a date. (Yes, I really do this.) More on this special date later. First, let's discuss why this is important.

We all have amazing intuitive powers. Unfortunately, many people don't tap into them. So often, we have urges, nudges, or inclinations to do something, but we ignore them. Thinking they're not meaningful. Especially when these urges encourage us to do something uncomfortable, taking an unknown path. As creatures of habit, it's easy to ignore our intuition when it's telling us to take a chance, even when it's something worth pursuing.

Those inklings come from your subconscious mind, but then the rational mind steps in and says, "*Oh no you don't.*" Especially when the idea seems unrealistic, or not what is normally done. Or beyond one's sense of self-worth.

But our gut feelings are important. I love listening to my intuition and seeing where it takes me creatively. An easy way to start is by paying attention to your intuition when it comes to little projects. Harmless stuff. Got an inkling to buy one of those pretty coloring books for grownups? Great, do it! Your subconscious might be nudging you about something more important than coloring.

You must follow the path if you want to find out where it leads.

For me, this means going with my gut when it comes to writing stories. Whenever I feel an urge to follow a certain path, I go with it. Usually with no idea where I'll end up. As the author, I almost feel more like the reader, because I don't yet know where things are headed. The intuition leads me down twisty, windy roads that my rational mind never would've dreamed up. It doesn't mean I can't make changes later, but I always make weird connections whenever I listen to my intuition.

Of course, intuition is useful for more than just creating things. It's great for solving problems. It may be scary in the beginning, before you learn from experience that it's safe to trust your intuition. That's why I recommend getting to know your intuition in small, harmless ways. Like decorating, or with art projects, or cooking. Any time where the worst that can happen is that you learn another way *not* to do something.

Like when my husband tried using up leftover French toast as the bread for grilled cheese sandwiches. It didn't work. The squishy, eggy toast never got crispy. But it was worth a shot, and the results were still edible. Speaking of, did you know that eggnog works as batter for French toast? Or that spiked eggnog is a yummy, holiday-spiced substitute for Bailey's in coffee? These two innovations were harmless, intuition-inspired experiments that actually worked. Well, it turns out they were only new to us, but already known to the world, or at least to Google. That's ok, very few inventions have never been tried by anybody in the history of all humans!

When you befriend and learn to trust your intuition, it opens up a whole world for your creativity. Inspiration will come to you much more easily because it feels welcome and confident. When you give your intuition room to whisper and grow, you'll have more creativity in your life. And the more you get used to this, the louder your intuition gets. Or so it seems... you've really just learned to pay attention to the intuition that was already inside of you.

When you trust your intuition, following it increases your relaxation. We experience a form of stress when our intuition tells us to do something, and we ignore it. But when we let intuition have a seat at the table, we feel more relaxed because we feel more authentic, truer to ourselves... there's nothing quite like the peace that comes from having your heart and mind in sync when making a decision. It also increases your confidence.

It's a powerful feeling to experience all of this. But when you shut down your intuition and constantly tell it *no*, your gut tightens. That's not a fun feeling. It's like locking down your soul with a padlock and tossing the key into a river.

As a young woman, I didn't always listen to my intuition. That is, unless it was telling me *not* to do something. My mom was really good at reminding me to look out for "red flags." Such as when interviewing for a job. Or entering a relationship, she might screech, "Kristen, that's a red flag! Don't date him!"

But these lessons were always based in fear, pulling me away from danger. We never talked about *green flags*... the "go" signals... the intuitions you have about going *toward* something. Like taking a chance on something that's important to you. Or pursuing your goals and dreams, or using your intuition to expand your creativity. But your *non*-fear-based intuition is there! Waiting. Available. Ready to help you.

Back to Our Romantic Date...

How can you use your intuition to help with creativity? Again, you ask your intuition out on a date, which I'll describe momentarily. And once you're there, in that mental frame, you do your Wine Self-Talk. The script below is designed to get you excited about using your intuition, and opening up your mind and heart to receive it.

The next important thing is to make time for *hearing* your intuition. You do this with *quietness*. Take 10 or 20 minutes, a few times a week, and just relax, paying attention to the feelings in your gut when you're thinking about your life in general. Or something in particular. It can be anything... diet, health, finances, your job, or even trivial stuff, like what Netflix show to binge on next! Seriously, it doesn't have to be something life-changing, and baby steps help get the ball rolling and start to establish a habit.

Here's how to do the date with your intuition:

First, pour your glass of wine. Take a few sips, and wait until you start to feel the wine's soft, warm feeling envelop you. When you feel it, for whatever insights you seek, imagine you are speaking directly to your intuition, and ask about the thing you seek in the form of a question:

Should I do _____?

Which _____ should I _____?

Where should I _____?

How should I go about doing ______?

And so on.

And then pay close attention to the *first thought that comes to mind.*

Whatever pops into your head, no matter how strange or seemingly unrelated, take a long, hard look at it. It might be a word, or a phrase, or an image. Or a memory. Maybe it will be the clear, straightforward answer you seek. Or sometimes, the thought that pops into your head is not so obvious, or it might seem irrelevant. Whatever it is, don't dismiss it! Instead, run with it, and go wherever it takes you, like you're following your spirit animal through misty woods in a dream, eager to discover what it's trying to show you.

Allow the thoughts in your head to run around, without restriction.

Next, take another sip of wine. Close your eyes, and pay attention to the feeling in your gut. Focus on the *emotions* more than the content of the thoughts.

Do the sensations feel expansive, playful, or encouraging? Sometimes, the insight comes as a strong *knowing*. Other times, it's a softer nudge to pursue some *thing,* and see where it goes. Sometimes it's a feeling of love. Or warmth. Or well-being.

Sometimes, you might feel a sense of unease. Or fear! And I don't mean when you feel nervous or scared because of the unknown, but scared because *you know better, and you should run!*

Through this process, I've gotten to know my intuition's feelings very well. It took some practice, but really, it just means paying attention to your emotions. Maybe even naming them, just to make things very clear.

When I feel excited about an idea for a product or a book, my stomach does somersaults, like I'm on a roller coaster (which I love). The feeling is juicy, enticing.

The feeling of knowing whether something is a good idea or not in business can also present itself as a sense of relaxed calm. For example, when a certain company approached me with a business proposition, I was initially interested. But I realized that my interest had more to do with my ego than anything else. Pursuing this opportunity would have closed other doors. There were lots of things to consider, and, on paper, it wasn't clear if it would be wise to proceed or not.

However, my intuition knew!

The deal wasn't right for me. My husband and I crunched numbers all kinds of ways to see if it made sense financially, but spreadsheets only get you so far... there are intangibles that don't have a dollar value, such as the impact on freedom and lifestyle. My intuition was *screaming* to say no. So I decided against accepting the offer. And the moment I made that decision, a wave of calm washed over me.

Instant proof!

Proof that I had made the right decision. I sent an email, politely declining the offer.

In hindsight, we hadn't needed to crunch the numbers. The feeling in my gut was all I needed to know. The financial analysis really just satisfied my practical side. The funny thing is, doing the analysis stressed me out. Because, the longer it took to make my decision, the more pissed off my intuition was getting because I wasn't listening to her! I had to chuckle at that... she can be feisty!

~

Use the following script to squeeze the most out of your luscious intuition...

Wine Self-Talk Script: Falling in Love with Your Juicy Intuition

My intuition is an important part of me, and I listen to it.

I pay attention to the feelings in my body, because they guide me on exciting paths.

I go on joyrides with my intuition, and she expands my creativity.

I laugh all the time, and it fills my body with bubbly effervescence.

Creativity is mine. I'll always have it. It's always swirling in me and through me, regardless of its form.

I love my intuition, and she loves me back.

I give my intuition time, quiet, and space to speak to me. I listen to her whispers. I smile at her roars.

I build my own fire inside of me, and my intuition strikes the match. I am magical. I am amazing. I am beyond.

We are one, all of us, always one. Connected. Our hearts full of love, hand to hand, helping one another, lighting a path around the world. I know this fully. I know this intuitively.

I look at myself, into my own face, into my own eyes, down into my own beautiful soul. I have a spark inside there, I see it. It's ready to WHOOOSH into existence. It fuels the rest of my days with knowing, intuition, power, and confidence.

I glow with dazzling charisma.

I show up to my life. Every day, I show up.

I come prepared, raring to go, excited with intuition and confidence.

Each day, my instincts bring amazing new surprises.

I am interesting.

I trust my feelings.

My intuition is fun, quick, and cool. It's like a sixth sense, clairvoyance, a magical knowing.

Sparks of inspiration and intuition turn to fire in my belly. The flames roar, and my creativity soars.

I am wildly abundant with life, riches, love, and magical living. My intuition is a special part of this grand design.

I show up to my life, confidence swirling around me in glittering wisps, like magical, white fire.

My intuition is the solution.

There is always more than enough for me because abundance is all around.

Creativity plays in every corner of my mind.

I am worthy of my desires. We are all worthy of our desires.

I love my intuition relentlessly. We are buddies. We are there for each other.

Creativity Tip: Move for Creativity

Don't freak out... I'm not talking about moving your residence. (Though big change like that can trigger massive creativity!)

Our minds all have an unfathomable number of ideas and memories just sitting there, hanging out, waiting just beyond the edge of consciousness. The formula for genius is pretty simple: Tap into those things, and make connections between them.

So, if you want to make it easier for those things to crisscross, connect, and bump into each other, then you must do things that support making these associations happen. You must put yourself into an *associative state*.

And one of the best, easiest ways to do that is... *go for a walk!*

That's right, move your body. Don't listen to an audiobook or podcast on your walk, just move your body, and the motion will automatically inspire intuition and creative flow. When I go for walks, there's something utterly freeing in my mind, like something has been unlocked. The movement of my legs, the passing of the earth beneath my feet, it's mesmerizing, and it opens all kinds of doors and ideas in my mind.

> *The moment my legs begin to move, my thoughts begin to flow.*
>
> — Henry David Thoreau

So, if you feel stuck on any problem or situation in your job, or business, or relationships, or artistry, or just your life, *take to the street, and move your feet.*

CHAPTER 13

WINE SELF-TALK SCRIPT: IMAGINATION TREASURE CHEST

> *Our most valuable resources—creativity, communication, invention, and reinvention—are, in fact, unlimited.*
>
> — David Grinspoon

At its most basic level, creativity is simply making connections that you don't normally make in your regular, more narrowly focused world. And you can make this easier by having more things to connect. Such as having more unique experiences to make connections between. More skills, more hobbies, more passions, more knowledge, more books you've read... basically, the stuff you learn when you get out into the world and try new things. Constantly. All of them give you more material to work with.

Take some time, right now, and think about combining something you already do with something you *don't* ordinarily do.

Is this a riddle? What do you mean, Kristen?

Let's use cooking as an example. Most of us cook, right? At least, a little? Now put a different spin on it to create a brand-new experience.

Perhaps cooking something from a cookbook featuring some exotic, new cuisine. Maybe it's adding M&Ms to cottage cheese. Or mustard to brownies. Perhaps it means cooking a meal with your spouse as your sous chef while playing music. Perhaps it's baking a big batch of chocolate chip cookies, and then sharing them with all of your neighbors on the street, even the ones you've never met.

The Toast Party

Here's another spin on doing something novel with food... host a themed party! Or make it a party with only one kind of food prepared a bunch of different ways. I once hosted a Toast Party. Not the clinking glasses kind; I literally served toast. I love toast—it's one of my favorite foods—so I thought, *"Why not have a party featuring all kinds of toast?"* I sent out invitations featuring a drawing of toast. The funny thing was, everyone thought Greg and I were making some big announcement, and they all asked in their RSVPs, *"What are we toasting to?"*

"Nothing. It's just toast," I'd say. "Really. We're eating toast. And drinking wine."

Everyone got a kick out of it. I bought a bunch of fresh sourdough bread from the farmer's market. I then toasted it and served it with a buffet of toppings: salted butter, beet hummus, wildflower honey, chocolate sauce, tuna salad, guacamole, pickled red onions, grape jelly, peanut butter, chocolate chips, banana slices, and more.

So, consider throwing your own weird, themed party. Not toast necessarily, but something that everybody likes, but nobody ever throws a dedicated party for. If not food, then perhaps some other fun but unusual activity.

Like this idea I heard from Tim Ferriss' podcast, when guest Chris Sacca shared the following:

> *Mullet wigs change everything. I was at a party recently, a good buddy of mine's 50th birthday party, and the crew he had there was a mix of people, some were serious business associates, others are really fun, aggressive, party people, there are some athletes, some artists, there are all walks of life, different cultures, too. I brought a bag of 75 or so mullet wigs, and I just opened it up, and I laid them out on a couch off to one of the sides of the party.*

He goes on to talk about how people started putting them on, and what a crazy-fun time everyone had.

Your Imagination Treasure Chest

When you expand your experiences and skills, you fill your *Imagination Treasure Chest* with more sparkling gems that enhance your creativity. It makes perfect sense... as you do more different things, you have more raw materials to draw from.

Look for ways to give yourself different experiences from everyday things. Grocery shopping, for instance. It's something you do anyway, but try out different stores, even specialty stores that might take longer to get to. When I lived in Michigan, I used to love driving the 30 minutes it took me to get to some of the best health food stores in Ann Arbor or Rochester. Or maybe the next time you go for pizza, try a different place. Maybe it's eating a keto diet for five days. Remember, when you expand your experiences—no matter what they are—you expand the pool of knowledge that your creativity draws from.

And do some things you never imagined yourself quite enjoying, but you do it, anyway, *just to add to your experience repertoire.* Perhaps it's going to a museum, even if you normally think of museums as boring. Or maybe you attend a country music concert, or the symphony, even though you're a die-hard rocker (or vice versa).

Maybe it's horseback riding lessons. Maybe it's volunteering at an animal shelter.

Maybe it's simply reading a sci-fi novel when your usual go-to is romance. Maybe it's watching a romantic comedy because it's something you'd normally never do. Maybe it's watching a hockey game or football when you know nothing about the rules. Maybe it's going bowling or playing billiards when you haven't done that in decades. It doesn't matter. It becomes a learning experience, and a new gem in your Imagination Treasure Chest.

Or try something new with your fashion. Consider wearing high heels with your frayed jean shorts, or sandals with your suit. Or put your hair in a sideways ponytail, like Chrissy in *Three's Company.* Or do something daring with your makeup! Whatever it is, do something... *anything*... the point is just to try something new!

You might not immediately know how some new experience is going to impact your creativity, or how it's going to improve your life. Perhaps it causes you to meet a new friend who expands your horizons. Perhaps a quick search for something online sends you down a three-hour Wikipedia rabbit hole, and you discover a whole new passion you didn't even know existed. Or perhaps you're just seeding your mind with new experiences that flower in the future.

What often happens is that, one day, you're doing something seemingly unrelated, and this new thing you tried recently tickles in the back of your mind, and then you suddenly make a crazy new connection, and this new connection takes you in a whole new direction, whether it's something small but interesting, or completely life-changing.

The Experts Game

Ok, so I know you're already convinced of how all these new experiences can increase your imagination. And you're already champing at the bit to make a list of things you can start playing around with. But first, I want to share one more tip. It's about the *Experts Game.*

According to research psychologist Robert Epstein,

New ideas come from interconnections among old ideas.

Epstein says we can take advantage of this by something called the *Experts Game*, in which you seek to learn about *obscure topics* in *small doses*.

In the Experts Game, you take a few people with extensive knowledge in widely differing topics. Each person gives a 5-minute lecture on something related to their area of expertise. After the talks are completed, the audience members are asked to come up with a new product or service that combines two of the topics covered in the lectures.

For example, if the experts talked about obscure topics like wooden bat houses, custom-made shoes, and biohacking with stem cells, then you would try to come up with a way to combine two of those topics into something useful.

It may seem crazy, but groups that Epstein has run through this game came up with "mind-boggling" ideas that would never have entered their imagination without the mini-lectures.

How can you take advantage of this?

Choose three unrelated topics and learn about them. Epstein says, "The more interesting and diverse the pieces, the more interesting the interconnections." So don't jump to looking up things that you already know something about, or have an interest in, or that you've always been curious about. Go after something totally random that you never thought about exploring. How do you pick something randomly? Easy, just point your web browser to:

https://en.wikipedia.org/wiki/Special:Random

It will take you to a random Wikipedia article. Try it, it's fun! Do it a few times to come up with your list of topics.

Is video more your thing? No problem, just go to:

https://random-ize.com/random-youtube/

It will take you to a random YouTube video.

Or perhaps ask a friend or family member to name a few random subjects, and then you go watch videos about them. Short videos are fine, 5-10 minutes each.

When you're done watching the videos, try to come up with a way to combine two of the topics. It could be an invention, no matter how impractical it seems. It can even be completely absurd... that's fine. The point isn't to actually make the thing, it's to give your brain a chance to practice combining things in novel ways. To get the ball rolling, sometimes I start with a question like, "Wouldn't it be cool if somebody invented a thing that did ____ and ____?"

Or maybe think of a way to combine two of the topics in a short story. What a great way to inject originality into storytelling!

It's ok if you're unable to come up with anything interesting. You're still massively exercising your creativity muscle when you do this exercise!

Wine Self-Talk Script: Imagination Treasure Chest

I increase my imagination muscle, I look for patterns, I make connections.

It's so fun to play with my imagination and see how far I can take it.

I am living the most amazing life, and I'm filled with gratitude.

I take time to learn more, try more, taste more, and experience more.

I grab inspiration by the handful. I stuff it into my pockets, and it's always there, whenever I need it. Things always work out for me.

I relax under the big, open sky. It's blue, and the sun's rays pour into me. I'm recharged. I am filled with so many imaginative ideas that I want to run, jump, dance, and do cartwheels.

My Imagination Treasure Chest is filled with all sorts of cleverness, from unconventional ideas, to genius ideas, to enterprising ideas, to unusual ideas. I mix and match them, and I come up with even bigger thoughts.

I'm a visionary!

I taste the mystery. I like its flavor. My imagination is full of rainbow life.

I love trying new things and working on new skills. It gives me more grist for my imagination mill.

My heart and soul are elevated. I am filled with a cool, clear, calm, like air after the rain.

I am inspired by everything. The moon, the flowers, the mosquitos, parrots, bees, my neighbors, pizza, traffic! I use my imagination to find inspiration in it all!

Everywhere I look, I see new connections.

My imagination expands every day. It grows like pixie dust is sprinkled all over it, coating it in shimmering gold.

I am grateful for my enormous imagination. It's filled with gems of every kind.

I am love. I love love. Love fills my imagination.

My brain is powerful. I love to learn. I love to expand my thoughts into new territories where I've never been before. It's electrifying. It's exhilarating.

We are all capable of using our powerful imaginations to spark ideas for making the world a more magnificent place.

Everywhere I look, I see something to boost my imagination.

I am filled with successful ideas. So many!

I am ready for creativity. I am proud and excited. I am on the edge of something wonderful and huge. I am living the best life ever. Yes! Yes! Yes!

I am happy. I am grateful for taking time to let my imagination blossom. It makes my life so incredibly fun.

I am worthy of living my best life. A life full of vigor, excitement, happiness, and glory.

I love having such a cosmically huge imagination. Thank you, imagination. Thank you, Me.

Creativity Tip: Change Your Surroundings

A really great way to inspire more ideas and creativity is to simply change your surroundings. That can mean moving from working at home to working in a cafe. It can be finding a different place to work, at work. If neither of these are possible, would you believe that your creativity can be sparked simply be rearranging your desk? Try a new chair, or adding a plant, or a candle, or changing which direction your desk faces. All of these things disrupt the patterns in your brain, taking you off the well-worn mental pathways, and can inspire insights and new ways of looking at old problems.

CHAPTER 14

WINE SELF-TALK SCRIPT: HUGGING YOUR OPPONENTS

> *I never made one of my discoveries through the process of rational thinking.*
>
> — Albert Einstein

Have you ever found yourself only reading books, or blogs, or news media that support your own opinion?

I'm raising my hand here. That was me a decade ago, when I was a vegan. And doing so almost killed my family. Ok, I'm being dramatic. Maybe.

At the time, I thought I was doing the right thing. Don't we always? I filled my life with all things vegan, following experts, reading book after book. Did I consume any information to the contrary? No, I didn't want to hear it. I wouldn't even entertain it. As far as I was concerned, the experts and scientists I was reading were truth, and the others were misguided, or worse, corrupted by conflicts of interest.

The result of my one-sided analysis? My family's health suffered because of my cognitive biases. One in particular, called *confirmation bias*.

Confirmation bias is when people create their own reality bubble by filtering out inputs from the world that disagree with their beliefs. In other words, we tend to ignore or discount things that don't fit with our model of reality, even to the point of defensiveness and digging in our heels. We all do this to varying degrees. It's normal. But some of us do it more than others, especially about specific topics. Sacred cows that we're not really interested in having disproven. It turns out, our sacred cows—things we believe with absolute certainty—are the things that we should periodically revisit, to see if they still make sense.

This error in thinking everything is a certain way can affect your rationality and cause you to make bad decisions. For the purposes of this book, it puts a stranglehold on your creativity.

It stifles our ingenuity if we never expose ourselves to opposing views, other opinions, experiences, thoughts, ideas, and beliefs. If we get all of our information from one source, then we won't know about other points of view. We keep everything as is, no new concepts or connections. No adventurous living.

My own confirmation bias guided my vegan research. And every time I read something that supported everything I believed, because I wanted to believe in a 100% plant-based diet—because *I love animals so damn much*—I would think, *See? See? There's the proof!* I was brash and cocky, and I looked down my nose at people who didn't "get it."

Well, the joke was on me when I ate sixty tons of humble pie. Turns out, my family suffered on a plant-based diet, despite it being well-planned, thoroughly researched, and augmented with thousands of dollars' worth of supplements. I still remember the day my toddler daughter started having problems walking. It scared the ever-loving crap out of me, and had me scrambling for a solution, frantic, willing to try anything. Even things that I previously never would have considered. Adding animal-based products to her diet immediately solved the problem, thank god.

When I look back to photographs of her prior to that, I see now, with the clarity of hindsight, that she had not been thriving. She looked gaunt and malnourished, but I wasn't able to see it at the time, such was my blindness caused by my cognitive biases. I'm relieved that I changed course in time to avoid permanent developmental problems. But damn... the guilt haunted me for years.

I swore I would never let my biases ever let me make that kind of mistake again.

As a result, I now make it part of my standard operating procedure to consider points of view that are different from my own, and with an open mind.

I read somewhere that the mind is like a parachute... if you want to survive, *it needs to be open!*

Since learning this lesson, I've cultivated an open curiosity, and it actually opened my mind to considering far-out possibilities, things that most people might dismiss out-of-hand. Such as living abroad. Or seeking dual U.S./Italian citizenship. At one point, I even experimented with eating a strict carnivore diet (eating only meat). But, unlike my vegan days, I did so with a wide-open mind, and this time, I didn't shout through a megaphone, telling people this was the only way.

We all have cognitive biases... even the psychologists who've spent their lives studying them. The thing that makes cognitive biases so sneaky for the rest of us is that they're mostly unconscious, so we don't know to do otherwise. That is, until we get burned... and that's not what I want for you.

There is another way. We may all have cognitive biases, but we can limit their impact somewhat by creating a few rules of thumb for ourselves. For instance, before committing to a big decision we're excited about, just to make sure we're not deluding ourselves, it's a good idea to consider alternatives, or list things that could go wrong. After doing these, if you still feel good about moving forward, then great... you're now moving forward with your eyes wide open. And you might come up with a better plan because you've thought through things more.

Another rule of thumb, to avoid deluding yourself with cognitive biases, is what I call *Hugging Your Opponents.*

Hugging Your Opponents

To prevent these cognitive biases from ruling your thoughts, always ask yourself, *What do other people say about this?*

And don't just ask yourself... find out the answer! Look it up! Even if the answers you find end up being Looney Tunes, at least you'll know what the other side is saying. And, heck, in my own experience, if I really dig down into something, I'll usually find an opinion that makes me go, *Huh... I hadn't thought of that.* That doesn't always mean it'll change my mind, but it'll make me smarter about how I proceed.

I call this process of considering the other points of view *Hugging My Opponents.* In other words, listen to what the other side has to say.

You see, a hallmark of enlightened thinking is the ability to temporarily suspend your assumptions about something, and take the other side, to play devil's advocate, and debate a position from the opposite point of view.

Don't worry, as soon as you're done with the exercise, you can switch back to your old beliefs.

But if you can't describe the other person's point of view—in words that *they would agree* captures the essence of their opinion—then you don't really understand it. You must first understand a position before you can evaluate it. If you judge something before you understand it, you're not only wasting your time... sometimes you're going to be wrong.

You know who doesn't like you hugging your opponents?

Your *EGO!*

Why? Because your ego doesn't like to be wrong. At least, fragile egos don't. Strong egos like discovering when they're wrong, because they see it as a chance to get smarter.

For the same reason, poor leaders throughout history have said, "Here's the plan, now do it." Whereas the strong leaders said, "Here's a plan. Does anyone have any better ideas? If not, tell me all the ways it can fail, and how we can prevent them."

Of these two approaches, which general's plan would you rather follow into battle?

Here's a great rule of thumb in life:

Half of what I know is false.
I just don't know which half.

Ok, maybe it's not half, but nobody's right about everything, and this cute little saying will always keep you on your toes! It's about being humble, which really means *to remain teachable.*

Because, the moment you stop being teachable, you stop learning. And that's the death of creativity. And the end of growing as a human being.

A lot of uncool things happen in politics, but one of the hands-down, weirdest things we've ever done, as a species that would like to survive, is to vilify someone who changes their mind by calling them a "flip-flopper." I mean, what kind of lunacy suggests people should never change their minds? There's certainly a time for consistency—most of the time, perhaps—but not in the face of new information.

When someone questioned economist Paul Samuelson about a change in his views, he famously replied,

When the facts change, I change my mind. What do you do, sir?

And not just when the facts change. You should periodically change your mind about some things just because you think about them more. Or your priorities change. Or you evolve as a human. You know, gaining experience. That's not inconsistency; that's called growing older and wiser.

So crack open your mind to new ideas by breaking down restrictive walls... start by hugging your opponents! Expand your perspectives to include at least *understanding* other points of view, even if you don't agree. Explore that territory.

Steps like this train our minds to be less affected by our cognitive biases.

Or at least to know when they're affecting our judgment.

Let's talk about how this can make life more magical. Understanding our biases, and the biases of other people, is an incredible way to become more creative! When you allow other points of view into your life, even if it's just to sniff them like a dog, you allow new data points into your mind, and these can make for more new connections. New ideas. More options from which to choose. More possible solutions... which usually means *better* solutions. New inventions even! Better products! Better art!

Flashes of insight that break through your creative plateaus!

I take this mindset of entertaining opposing ideas with me everywhere I go. Whether it's politics, or food, or cultural differences, or... you name it. I believe I can learn from anyone... at least something. Everyone is an expert in something I know nothing about. I ask people questions and give them the space to express themselves. I keep my heart open to people who think differently than I do, because I never know what connections might spark in my brain as a result. I actively inquire, and I listen openly, with the goal of discovering something new. Not to confirm what I already think.

As a writer, this is immensely helpful for storytelling!

As an entrepreneur, it's super smart for coming up with new products, or services, or entire businesses. In fact, fun story, the idea for one of my top-selling books came straight from negative feedback in a reader's review! Someone gave *Coffee Self-Talk* a one-star review because she had expected it to be a daily reader. So what did I do? I published *The Coffee Self-Talk Daily Reader*... and it flew off the shelves!

Clearly, lots of other readers wanted something like that as well. As a businessperson, it would have been foolish of me to dismiss such important feedback.

But beyond these practical benefits—business, marketing, etc.—as a human, it helps my soul to be open to other people's ideas and beliefs. In fact, if everybody suddenly did this, right now, even just a little bit, the world would be, like, 50% better in about fifteen minutes. Not bad, huh?

When you start opening your mind like this, don't be surprised if, one day, you come up with a great idea that bridges two opposing points of view. Creativity is, after all, making new connections, and one of the best ways to have more opportunities for new connections is to increase, not only your data pool, but your data pool of things that are just sitting out there, *needing to be connected!*

So go ahead and engage people with opposing viewpoints, and ask all kinds of honest questions with an open heart, to see where they're coming from, and why. It doesn't mean you have to change your position, but you never know what might happen, including sparking your creative genius, or sparking understanding and love.

Wine Self-Talk Script: Hugging Your Opponents

I have an open mind, because having an open mind makes me more creative.

I come up with all kinds of cool ideas when I consider many points of view.

I'm brilliant, and I love to learn. That means grabbing my notebook and pen and jumping headfirst into life. I explore all terrains of thoughts, both mine and others'.

My ability to relax in all circumstances is one of my superpowers.

My needs will always be met. I am capable. I am safe. I am AWESOME!

Ideas fall into my lap, because I stay open and curious about everything.

My dazzling confidence in myself is astounding. I smile brightly and with ease.

I've fallen in love with keeping an open mind. It makes my life better in every possible way.

I am driven by the electricity of creativity. I thrive in an ocean of ideas.

Individuality is critically important. Yet we are still all connected. We are all one.

I press forward into the unknown, with curiosity and excitement lighting the way.

I love my magical life so much, I want to jump up and down on my bed. Living a creative life is a-mazing! I want to do cartwheels, tap dance, and fly.

I honor myself and my ideas. I also give others space to share their thoughts, and I learn from this. This makes my life even more dazzling.

I find different ways to do things all the time. Because my mind is open. My specialty is coming at problems from all different angles. Sliding in sideways, with brilliant ideas flowing from me.

I'm grateful for having an open mind. It fuels my fresh and innovative thinking. It's the only way to roll!

I am devoted to the exhilaration of uncertainty. I have the courage to let go of certainties.

I am overflowing with love, and I infuse my body with affection and appreciation.

Because my mind is open, original ideas come to me all the time. Like a bolt of lightning. Bam! Crackle! Shazam!

Whenever I hear something that sounds incorrect, I try to see things from the other person's perspective, and I ask myself how they might have come to believe it.

I love having both ears open to listen, both eyes open wide to see. I use my mouth to ask questions. I use my heart to be free.

I invent. I create. I tinker with contradicting ideas. I'm comfortable with uncertainty. I experiment. I grow. I take chances. I break boundaries. I'm constantly learning.

My open-minded creativity pierces the mundane, and I discover the illuminated marvelous. Wow, life is so incredible!

Creativity Tip: Practice Pattern Recognition

You can encourage creativity by paying attention to *patterns in what you observe.*

For example, if you watch a lot of movies, you might see that most movies rely on certain elements and structures, motifs, and tropes. For instance, "boy meets girl," or "fish out of water," or "slow-motion walking away from an explosion." And once you identify these patterns, you'll start to see them everywhere. Then, you can apply these patterns to other contexts (for instance, when giving a presentation at work), and see what cool ideas come from that.

Or perhaps you sharpen your pattern-recognition skills by paying attention to nature, like the birds nesting in your trees. Do you notice particular things that always happen? Can you discover what to expect? And how can you transfer this knowledge to something completely unrelated in your life?

Or perhaps the patterns of the seasons—what can you recognize about those? Henry David Thoreau did this when he made an analogy between the seasons and the parts of a day. He wrote,

> *The day is an epitome of the year. The night is the winter, the morning and evening are the spring and fall, and the noon is the summer.*

That's a creative connection!

CHAPTER 15

WINE SELF-TALK SCRIPT: INGENUITY EXPECTATION

Creativity is contagious. Pass it on.

— Albert Einstein

Every morning, the sun comes up.

When you click the light switch... the light always turns on.

When you turn the faucet... water always comes out.

When you ask your brain to do something clever... *does your brain always deliver?*

Wouldn't it be nice if your *inner genius* were as dependable as the sunrise, electricity, or water? And you never had to worry about whether or not you'd come up with the answers you need? If you could just trust that your creativity would always flow?

You should not be surprised when your brain delivers brilliance. You should come to expect it. Why? Because the *expectation* is part of what makes it happen.

When you're surprised at something brilliant you've done, that sends a message to your brain that this was a fluke. That it's not normal. That it's a rare occurrence, and you shouldn't come to expect it. Or depend on it.

In other words, when you treat your creative lightning as something special, it's a reaction based on an assumption of scarcity. Which is the opposite of what we're striving for here: an abundance of creativity.

You want your creativity to flow so much, so regularly, that it becomes commonplace. Like Superman zooming off with confidence, rather than looking down and going, *Whoa, am I really flying?*

When it comes to your creative genius, you want to *own it*. Like it's the most natural thing in the world for you. Brilliant ideas? Sparks of genius? Clever connections?

Yes, that's right, *all the time.*

Building Your Ingenuity Expectation

I wrote about the power of *expectation* in my book, *Pillow Self-Talk*. The context was about having an expectation about happiness. The idea here is similar. You want to cultivate an expectation that your inner genius is always there, always working for you, always generating ideas.

As a kid, did you ever make a Christmas wish list and know you'd receive something on the list? Or perhaps you had a grandparent who always sent you a check for twenty dollars on your birthday. In other words, you came to *expect* these things.

And because you expected it, you didn't stress about whether you would get it. You probably didn't even think too much about it. And it's with this idea that I want you to examine your expectations about your own creativity. We can take advantage of this "expectancy" feeling to develop a creativity mindset that delivers ingenuity, not just occasionally (or never), but consistently. Every day.

Think about it for a minute right now. Tap into the feeling you have about something you're looking forward to... maybe your birthday, or a holiday, or an upcoming trip... anything you *expect*, and you're excited about. Different people might feel it in different ways. For some, there might be a nice, gentle sense of calm. For me, it's more tingly. Is there a jazzy feeling in your chest? Or maybe it's shimmery. Or maybe you're bouncing up and down. Whatever it is, marinate in that emotion for a moment, and memorize that feeling!

Now, take that feeling, and apply it to your creativity. Take that knowing in your heart you felt a moment ago, and connect it with thoughts of expecting ingenuity, ideas, and creativity. They're all coming. Know it. Believe it. *Feel it.*

I go on and on about how important it is to sync your thoughts with your feelings, when it comes to manifesting your dreams, and this is one way to tap into that "feeling" part. When something seems difficult to imagine and feel, it's because it's foreign to you, and so you use a surrogate feeling of something you have experienced to fill the void. So, in this case, if you've never experienced the feeling of having never-ending creativity, no problem... just conjure some other feeling of certainty—it can be anything you're confident about—and then pull a little switcharoo in your head, and pretend that that's how you feel about your reliably genius inner mind.

And now that you're feeling this expectancy for creativity and ingenuity, keep going. Have faith in your brain's ability to make incredibly wild connections. Expect creativity to come easily to you. Believe that you'll always have a boatload of great ideas. Trust that you're magical, and powerful, and that you can manufacture originality on a whim, that the process is always working away in your brain, behind the scenes, while you sleep, while you cook, while you drive... while you do anything. *Just expect it!*

When you expect something to happen, you *believe* it's going to happen, and this invests more of your soul into seeing that outcome materialize. Belief makes it more likely to happen because you start to see things differently in the world. And most of all, you start to relax. Because, if you don't relax, you start to wonder, and then doubt, and pretty soon, you can get wound up in a cycle of tightness and anxiety.

But when you expect things to work out for you, when you expect prolific, flowing creativity to be a *foundational part* of your life, it's an incredibly relaxing experience. It's a *No worries, man, I got this* kind of energy, like the heroine in a movie whom everyone knows is gonna *kick ass*. Having a clear mind makes you relaxed, calm, and allows your thinking brain to take a step back and let your subconscious work its magic, as new ideas start to percolate and blossom.

Wine Self-Talk Script: Ingenuity Expectation

I'm a wild, churning river, full of ideas constantly washing through me like white capped waves.

My life is colorful, ignited by bold ideas on all sides.

I trust in life. I trust in my abilities to create and make the coolest connections.

I trust in my confidence. I believe in love, and peace, and adventure.

I open my creativity wings wide, ready for a wild ride.

I am curious, open-minded, and interested in what I am doing.

I have the courage to relax. I rest when I need to, and it sharpens my senses.

I speak my inspirations to life by saying them out loud in my self-talk. The universe listens. My brain focuses. I make amazing things happen!

I love exploring new things, and I'm constantly trying out new ideas. Seeing what sparks and takes root, and seeing what doesn't. Moving on. Dancing on. Always creating.

I surround myself with tools that inspire my inspiration and creativity. I am an effective creative, and I make amazing things.

Life is a party. My life is a party. I love life! It's a great, great day!

I expect great things to happen this week. My life is fantastic.

The more I focus my mind on the good, the more good comes rushing into my life.

I charge forward in life... big, buoyant, diamond-dazzling and proud. I own my power, my intelligence, my wisdom, and my creativity. I expect incredible things to happen all the time.

With each success I achieve, each step I take, I attract more success.

I am grateful for everything in my life. I wake up filled with sunshine in my soul.

I am a creative genius!

Ideas pulse in my mind, stories beat in my soul, inspiration swims through my veins. I'm an innovative genius. Thank you, me, for taking the time to allow my creativity to flourish.

I rest easy with expectations of success, because my creativity is a part of my life, all the time.

I flow from idea to implementation with ease. Step after step, it's a breeze.

I am worth all the time I want and need to be my best self. We are all worthy.

I understand that creativity comes easily to me. I smile knowingly. Ideas are here. Connections are being made. I'm ready for it all. Bring it on!

Creativity Tip: Routines for The Creative Win

If you create a morning routine that you can slide into easily, it'll let you tap into the "flow" mode we often wake in. Because morning routines are automatic, you do them without thinking. Which means there are no disruptive beta brainwaves to mess with your mojo.

When I wake up, the first thing I do—after getting my coffee, of course—is plop my butt down in my special *Juju Corner* (see Chapter 10), where I do my Coffee Self-Talk, I journal, and I read. Then, I slide over to my desk, and I keep the flow going by using my automated, routine motions to transition into my work: writing. I just sit down and begin. I slip into it easily, and this frees my brain up for maximum creativity. My mind flies, wide open, and ready to receive.

Routine, in an intelligent person, is a sign of ambition.

— W.H. Auden

CHAPTER 16

WINE SELF-TALK SCRIPT: WATERFALLING IDEAS

> *There are five basic tastes, yet combinations of them yield more flavors than can ever be tasted.*
>
> — Sun Tzu, *The Art of War*

Ideas... they're like little puffs of magical breath. Precious, golden energy in a form you can't see... that is, until you transform the idea from energy into matter. Ideas make life thrilling, gleaming, and exciting. To hold an idea in your mind can be more magnificent than any possession you can hold in your hand. Yet, even all those possessions were once ideas too! *Ideas! Ideas! Ideas!*

Such a fun way to live, coming up with ideas. Ideas make life easier when they solve problems. They make people happy when you use them to help others. They make beauty when you create art. They make money when you make things you can sell.

So, how can you come up with more ideas? First, it bears repeating... you *can* cultivate creativity.

Creativity is a learnable skill.

Anyone can learn to do it. And to help this process along, you need to make creativity a habit.

In the book, *Where Good Ideas Come From*, author Steven Johnson says that coming up with good ideas requires looking at the "spare parts" in your life and reassembling them to come up with new ideas. In other words, if you take a couple of small appliances apart and put all the pieces on a table, what new things can you make by rearranging them? The trick isn't to dream up big thoughts all the time. Sometimes, the trick is simply getting more good "parts on the table" to use. So, how do you do get more parts on the table?

Getting More Parts

Below is a list of neat ways to help you get more *parts on the table* for combining in new ways. Once you start adding to what's available in your mind to work with, you'll be amazed at the neat, new connections you're able to make.

1. Expand Your Interests

Find a new hobby. You never know what having a new hobby could do for your creativity in areas that lie outside of the hobby itself. For example, taking a cooking class might give you an experience that, strangely, makes you more successful when helping someone at work who's having a problem. Learning to sew might come in useful when camping in the great outdoors. In fact, anytime a hobby requires that you learn how to use a new tool—whether it's an X-ACTO knife, a hot glue gun, or some new software application—it's remarkable how you'll suddenly start finding ways to use that new tool in totally unrelated contexts. Enough to make you say, *How did I ever get by without this?*

2. Meet New People in New Surroundings

Go on a bus tour of your town with strangers, or a Segway tour, or join a pub crawl, or do a food-n-drink tour in a town an hour away from you. Chat up the people you meet there, ask questions, get curious. Be a tourist! Have fun! The point is meeting new people and opening your eyes to new things. Look to your local library or university for free talks and events. Check out local cafes for open mic nights, and go to just hang out and meet other people.

3. Seek Out Unique Environments

Take your daily walk, but instead of taking your usual route, mix it up and walk a different path that you've never walked before. Or, once a week, go do your daily walk someplace special, such as a historic area of your town, or a zoo, or botanical gardens. You'll get two birds with one stone here: exercise plus a new environment. Keep in mind, studies show that natural settings can boost creativity. Things like trees, sunshine, water, flowers, birds, etc.

Think of your own office surroundings and get quirky with changing it up. Maybe you hang a super weird piece of art on the wall. Maybe you paint rainbows or polka dots on the ceiling. Hang beach balls from the corners of the room. Put a basket of rocks on your desk, or fruit, or yarn. If you have a couch in your office, fill it with your kids' stuffed animals for a couple of weeks. The point is to have unusual things in your environment to take you out of an overly familiar mental state, which will help you spark unusual ideas. Pro-tip: change things up once a month.

4. Develop Your Current Talents

Level up your current skills. If you're good at singing, take a class to develop your voice further, such as to record a song or perform live. If you're proficient at Spanish, try out for a play with a role that speaks Spanish. If you're a writer, take a class on poetry, or comedy.

If you're handy around the house, improve your skills by taking on an ambitious project... something that's just at the edge of your capabilities, such that you'll have to learn and grow. Such as building a deck or a gazebo, or doing some landscaping.

5. Seek the Ridiculous

Go nutty with your thinking, and try to figure out how to train your cat to use the toilet (this is a real thing... there are even kits that help kitties flush!). Or how to get your dog to dust the floor. Or how to recycle cowboy boots into furniture. The idea is getting *waaaay* out there with seemingly impossible things, just to get the creative juices flowing. You may not actually succeed in these things (but hey, who knows)... but that's not the point. The point is to get you thinking outside the box, which builds your creativity muscle.

6. Intentional Wandering

Intentional wandering refers to a special type of aimless exploration, into new places, or doing new things, or simply following your curiosity into new topics on the Internet, with the key feature being that your wandering does not have a specific goal in mind other than *to wander*. You don't start out looking for a specific answer. You're simply taking a break from normal living to explore. To wander. There is no pressure on yourself here.

> *Not all who wander are lost.*
>
> — J.R.R. Tolkien

Although this was intuitive to me, I didn't make it a regular activity until author Malcolm Gladwell pointed it out as something he does to find new topics to write about.

As he describes the concept, you have to remove the pressure of productivity from yourself, and feel free to go down roads that don't necessarily lead anywhere. At least, not initially. Just go for a wander, and see what you discover—facts, stories, ideas, thoughts, opinions—and tuck them away on a back shelf in your mind. When you do enough of these little wanderings, you soon acquire a shelf packed with a bunch of cool little pearls.

Then, be patient, and let things percolate in the background, with no intention, no goals, and no inkling of how any of these things might pay off some day in the future. The bigger the collection, the better the odds that something will be useful at some point. When you have acquired more diverse experiences and knowledge, it makes the soil in your brain fertile ground for growing new connections.

According to the author, Neil Gaiman,

> *You get ideas from daydreaming. You get ideas from being bored. You get ideas all the time. The only difference between writers and other people is writers notice when we're doing it. You get ideas when you ask yourself simple questions. The most important of the questions is just, 'What if...?'*
>
> *What if you woke up with wings? What if your sister turned into a mouse? What if you all found out that your teacher was planning to eat one of you at the end of term, but you didn't know who?*

Three Silly Ideas

If you want to come up with more ideas on a regular basis, it takes practice. You need to strengthen that *idea muscle* inside your head. After doing the exercises listed above, you'll have a lot of great stuff for your mind to work with, and now, it's time to practice. Make ideation second nature by practicing coming up with ideas. No matter how silly, initially.

And when I say silly, I mean *silly*:

- *A love story where jelly must decide between peanut butter and Nutella*
- *A device that uses hair snarls from a hairbrush to entertain cats*
- *A dating app for fans of the '90s TV show, Northern Exposure*
- *... and so on.*

The idea is to crank out so many ideas, without judgment, that your brain just starts doing it habitually. Through our good friend, repetition, your brain fires and wires, until thinking up new ideas, *all the time*, is simply part of your personality.

I love the following daily exercise, inspired by author, hedge-fund manager, and serial entrepreneur, James Altucher. He recommends that you create a list of *ten ideas every day*. Here's the secret, though... there's no restriction on how *bad they are*. In fact, the sillier the better, because it opens you up to just let 'em rip.

Altucher actually calls the exercise "Ten Shitty Ideas" to drive home the point, but I dropped the *shitty*, for better self-talk. I also started with only three ideas a day initially, as opposed to Altucher's ten. When I attempted ten, I found it too daunting, and I didn't come up with any. It took too much effort, so I didn't even start.

That said, his reasoning for ten makes sense. He stresses that, by forcing yourself to come up with so many ideas, it forces you to come up with even sillier ones—it lowers the bar—because that's what happens when you're pressed to generate ideas *in quantity*. In fact, he goes on to say that, if you can't generate 10, then you're trying too hard, and you should instead generate 20! That is, increasing the number will actually reduce the pressure to make the ideas good. *"Perfectionism is the enemy of the idea muscle,"* he says. So whether you start with a daily habit of a few ideas or 20, go for it. Just start. That's more important than the number you choose.

Figure out what works for you. Lowering my daily quota to three ideas made it much easier for me to be consistent. And it was fun. (Trust me, mine were still plenty silly.) Over time, I increased my number to five, and eventually, I got to the point where I would often do ten a day easily. So feel free to start small, even just writing down one silly idea per day. If you stick with it, you'll soon start coming up with more.

The reason that happens is because you are exercising your idea-generating muscle. Anytime you do something repeatedly, it gets easier to do. Those pathways in your brain start to wire, and your brain gets faster at grabbing information from different regions and connecting them in new ways. The crazy thing is that it applies to all kinds of tasks beyond coming up with items for your daily *silly ideas* list. Such as new ways to combine ingredients, or putting different clothing together, or solving problems at work, or in other areas of your life.

> *Ideas are like rabbits. You get a couple and learn how to handle them, and pretty soon you have a dozen.*
>
> — John Steinbeck

Your ideas can be about anything. And they might not even be silly. (The "silly" part is just to make it easy; good ideas will also sometimes come up.) You can make lists of:

- TV shows you'd like to see made
- Restaurants you wish existed
- Videos you can make
- People you can introduce to each other
- Crazy sandwiches you can make
- Things you want to see invented
- Ways you can save time
- Ways you can save money
- How to make jewelry from recycled plastic straws
- Household products needing improvement
- Etc.

You get the idea... have fun with these idea lists!

I have a tab in my journal where I keep my daily ideas list. And because I journal every day, right after I do my Coffee Self-Talk, I simply open my journal and list my ideas right then and there. This is not an activity you want to spread throughout the day. It's much more impactful if you sit down and let your brain start to flow. 1, 2, 3... *go!*

And once you get these ideas out of your mind and onto paper, it frees up space in your mind. For more ideas!

Now, if one of your ideas shines to you, or keeps popping into your mind later on, then you might want to add it to a new list of "good ideas," perhaps grouped by category. And even those ideas can be silly; they just need to be interesting enough that you might want to revisit them later, and possibly take action on one or more of them. But, just to be clear, good ideas are just a nice by-product of this daily habit. The point isn't to eventually come up with a million-dollar idea; it's to get very comfortable at coming up with *many* ideas *all the time*. So many, in fact, that you come to see yourself as so good at generating ideas, that ideas themselves become abundant, not scarce. That's the whole point. Just come up with ideas.

Bottom line: Ideas are abundant, and you'll truly experience this by exercising your idea muscle with daily practice.

Wine Self-Talk Script: Waterfalling Ideas

I love coming up with new ideas, and it happens all the time.

Ideas roll through me like ocean waves, getting bigger and more powerful as they go.

I'm an idea creation machine. Ideas crank and churn inside me constantly.

I am amazing. I am profound. I am love. I am energy. I am living my most legendary life.

I am full of kindness for myself and kindness for others. I see strangers walking by, and I gush waterfalls of love to them, to you, to me.

I plant ideas inside me. They're seeds. I nourish and grow them with love and passion. Then, I harvest them, a bountiful basket of ideas spread out before me.

I trust my feelings. They come from my inner genius, and they nudge me in the right direction.

New concepts, plans, and designs pop into my head all the time. So many, I grab my notebook and jot them down. One, after another, after another. A waterfall of ideas, ongoing and ongoing. It's amazing.

Ideas dance their way around me. They dance through me, bobbing and swirling.

I love trying new things because it gives me new ideas.

I constantly expand my interests, which plants more seeds for new ideas.

Ideas come at me from all directions. Sideways, from above, from near and far. They're there! And there! Oh, and over there! Ideas are everywhere!

Each day brings amazing new ideas, fun, and excitement. Adventure is my jam. It's my juice in my legendary life!

I am abundant, flush with creativity, thoughts, and ingenuity. I have the time to explore everything I want. Time is abundant.

I am worthy of explosive, crazy-cool ideas. My thoughts are full of originality. I make connections and sprout new concepts all the time. It's just who I am.

I'm clever, curious, and I see possibilities everywhere I turn. My creativity rumbles in my bones.

I'm wide awake. I'm alert with self-love. I'm open to all the new ideas running around my head, right now and always.

I have a phenomenal brain and memory. I remember everything I want to remember.

I am happy! I am happy! I am happy, happy, happy!

Creativity Tip: Exercise with Music

When you exercise, listening to music can improve your creativity. In one study, researchers tested people on their verbal fluency after exercising with and without music. The results showed that, when the subjects listened to music while working out, their verbal fluency scores more than doubled! The study's lead author speculates that the combination of music and exercise stimulates cognitive arousal, which can assist in organizing cognitive output.

Many people already listen to music while exercising, but *knowing* about these interesting research findings can make the effect more powerful because it causes you to *expect* this result.

CHAPTER 17

WINE SELF-TALK SCRIPT: FAILING FORWARD

> *Creativity is allowing yourself to make mistakes. Art is knowing which mistakes to keep.*
>
> — Scott Adams

Scott Adams, creator of the *Dilbert* comic wrote,

> *I have cultivated a unique relationship with failure. I invite it. I survive it. I appreciate it. Failure always brings something valuable with it.*

I particularly love when he wrote that he,

> *Grabs failure by the throat and squeezes it until it coughs up a hairball of success.*

What a phenomenal attitude to have about failing. I love it. In a strange way, it gets me *amped up to fail.*

I've definitely had my share of failures. I've had big ones and small ones. Big failures, such as my failure to get into medical school (I didn't study hard enough and got distracted by boys). And the failure of my first marriage... I didn't love myself, and I married someone who didn't really love me either. I've had sooo many recipe failures (blending sardines and heavy cream tastes as bad as it sounds—it's a long story as to why I even tried this). I could go on... ah yes, my famous epic fail with the vegan diet. World travel failures. Product failures. Website failures. Relationship failures.

But here's the thing. With each of those failures, I learned lessons that I will take with me for my entire life. Mistakes I will not make again.

But even more exciting is that some of those failures, especially the big ones, closed doors that allowed me to open other doors. So, although I didn't go to medical school, I got a high-paying corporate job. Win, right?

Well, that led me to being chronically overworked and crazy-level stressed out. Fail, right?

Well, the job was so demanding that I didn't have time to go out and socialize, so I used eHarmony to find a boyfriend, and we've been married over ten years! Success!

You just never know where the path will take you. There is a role for mistakes. They're a necessary part of the process. If you take a good look at your life, you'll see that it's riddled with failures of all different sizes, but here you are, still standing, still getting back up on that crazy-ass horse. (Mine's a pink Pegasus, of course). And with these failures, you make all future experiences better. It's like the failures are threads that get woven into the blanket of your life. In the end, that blanket protects you. Keeps you warm.

In this light, failure is kind of beautiful. It's a natural part of *life's flow*.

Here's another thing about the beauty of failing. You can even look at *other people's* failures and learn from *them*. Which, of course, means other people can learn from *your* failures. My daughter learns a lot when I talk to her about the failures I've had in relationships and business. It's not the same as going through the painful experiences herself, but whenever possible, it's better to learn lessons, as they say, "on someone else's nickel."

The same goes for me and my own mother. I've learned a lot from her mistakes. Many years ago, she owned a trucking business that ultimately failed, and to this day, I still carry those lessons she taught me.

Before we met, my husband cofounded a tech startup in Silicon Valley that ultimately failed, and the stress caused him to hit rock bottom. But once he recovered from that, he said everything else was so much easier that he felt "bulletproof." I mean, *nothing* fazed him. When we were married, I would get stressed about some dumb, random thing, and he was calm as a cool cat. I'd ask him how he managed not to be *freaking out* like me! He'd shrug and say, "I've been through worse. This is nothing." So his failure taught him not only perspective, but also a kind of emotional strength, which he then taught to me.

Some of the most incredible inventions have been made as a result of mistakes. In 1839, Charles Goodyear accidentally burnt a piece of rubber on a hot stove and discovered the vulcanization process by which tires are still made today.

In 1903, Edouard Benedictus accidentally dropped a flask containing cellulose nitrate in his lab. The glass flask shattered when it hit the ground, but it held its shape due to the substance coating the inside of the glass. And this is how he invented the laminated safety glass that's in your car's windshield today.

And Thomas Edison famously made over a thousand attempts before creating a light bulb that worked. When people asked him how he handled all those failures, he said, "Those weren't failures. I just learned a thousand ways not to make a light bulb."

So, if at first you don't succeed, try, try again, and be excited to be taking steps closer to your goal, with each passing attempt.

In 1874, William Stanley Jevons wrote,

> *It would be an error to suppose that the great discoverer seizes at once upon the truth, or has any unerring method of divining it. In all probability the errors of the great mind exceed the number those of the less vigorous one. Fertility of imagination and abundance of guesses at truth are among the first requisites of discovery; but the erroneous guesses must be many times as numerous as those that prove well-founded.*

Failures and mistakes are like magical tools, a sparkling screwdriver or a glittering hammer. They help you make better choices in the future. Failure is not the end; it's one of the steps on a process that ends in success.

In fact, if you take note of the failures in your life, I'll bet you can come up with a list of all kinds of lessons you've learned. Going forward, consider all failures in this light. Because, I promise, there's gold there.

Tips to Build the Failures-Are-Fabulous Skill

There's a thing called *retrospective judgment,* when naturally happy people put a positive spin on negative past experiences, so they remember them as good. Like someone who goes on vacation, loses her luggage, gets rained on most of the days, and had a raging case of Montezuma's Revenge after sipping the wrong glass of water... but when you ask how her vacation went, she says, "Awesome!" and proceeds to list all the positive things about it.

Retrospective judgment can be a smart way to view failures. Seeing the positive helps you learn by overpowering the negative memories that might otherwise drown out the lessons. Finding the silver linings will also help reduce your stress. So, from here on out, if you have a failure, you're going to take a new perspective:

Failure is fabulous because I'm going to learn from it.

This doesn't mean you forget what went wrong; it means you learn from it and appreciate the lesson.

I've had some success in life. And you know what? Most of my biggest successes came after correspondingly big failures. I married an incredible man (on the second try), I have a beautiful daughter (after a failed IVF attempt and miscarriage), I love the work I do (after having gone through many not-so-fun jobs). I'm not living a magical life *despite* these failures, I'm living a magical life *because of* these failures.

They were necessary for me to get where I am today.

There is no shortcut through life.

Failures are not the problem. It's *how you see* failures that makes the difference. And when you view failure in a way that isn't helpful, or holds you back, then you need to change how you see them. On the balance sheet of your mind, you want to convert your failures from *liabilities* into *assets*.

For everyone except a very lucky few, success requires that you learn a lot, and you keep learning. Pretty much for your whole life. Specifically, learning what works and what doesn't. When you learn something that works—it could be anything, from learning how to make sourdough bread, to running a business—that's great, count it as a success. But for every successful way to make a loaf of sourdough, or run a business, there are a thousand ways to mess it up! And nobody perfects their art without *exploring*, and exploring means finding both what works *and* what doesn't work.

We call the things that didn't work "failures," but that's unfortunate, because they're really just learning how not to do something, like Edison and his thousand light bulb attempts. The point is, *he did not give up!*

Grab a Fat Eraser and Celebrate Failure!

Almost nobody accomplishes anything truly difficult on the first try. If they do, it's luck. Luck is great, but you don't depend on it. No, you want dependable processes. Such as processes that assume *learning* is part of the plan. And plans that assume not everything will go according to the plan.

Jason Fagone wrote the book, *The Woman Who Smashed Codes*, about Elizebeth Smith Friedman, America's first female code-breaker. She and her husband solved puzzles to unmask Nazi spies and help win World War II. According to the book,

> *They liked pencils with soft lead and big erasers, the eraser end seeing as much action as the lead end.*

See? These two brilliant cryptanalysts *assumed* failures and mistakes as part of the journey to success. And when it's assumed from the beginning, and you just work your way through it anyway, can you even really call it failure? That makes no sense. It's not failure, it's forward progress. It's success!

So grab yourself a mega fat-ass eraser and go!

Now, I understand that, despite all the above, failure isn't fun. But rather than thinking of it as a setback, just think of it as *work*. Part of the slog. The kind where you say,

No way through it but to do it.

Even if it feels crappy in the moment, you'll kick butt the next time. And the more you do this, the easier it gets. In fact, I recommend you go so far as to *celebrate failures*. Why? Because they mark progress. I call it *failing forward*. For the BIG steps forward—the big-ass failures... the *doozies*—well, hell, go ahead and crack open a bottle of Champagne! (See Chapter 20!)

Bonus Time! Now that you are excited about this new way of understanding the failures in your life, and you can see the golden opportunities that they can present, you not only feel better about yourself, but—*get this*—you are now equipped to drop any need for perfectionism or any fear of embarrassment.

Imagine... *no fear!*

Because, when you are not afraid to fail, you try more things. And you spend less time worrying about perfecting things, which means *more time for creating*. And you spend less time being scared or stressed, and more time having fun. You will go forward with peace of mind. And peace of mind is a powerful force for creativity.

~

Use the following script to rewire your brain to see failures as opportunities and steps toward progress. When you fall down, no problem... just pick yourself up, dust off the dirt, and get back on that gleaming Pegasus, and *fly, fly, fly!*

Wine Self-Talk Script: Failing Forward

When I make a mistake, I learn from it, then grab my big eraser and rub it away.

I love letting go of things that no longer serve me. It lightens my load. This puts bounce in my step, and I go, go, go!

If a roadblock comes up, I give it a wink. This is when I work best, busting through any kinks.

I strike a warrior pose, ready for anything that comes my way. A knowing smile, a twinkle in my eye, and learning every day.

Failures are diamonds in the rough. I dig to find them, loving the radiance they shine on my life.

Problems are part of the exciting game of life. Through each one, I become a better and smarter version of myself.

I rise above my past, stronger every day, growing every day, learning every day. I am spectacular. I was born for this life of magnificence. I am resilient.

Storms come and go, and I ride the rainbows after. Anytime I make a mistake, it always makes me better at my craft.

I go after problems, solving them with ease. I love my life.

My peace of mind is a mighty force driving my creativity.

Love. It's the answer to everything, no matter the slips, trips, or falls. Love makes me stand tall. I survive, and I thrive. Watch me go!

I am peaceful. I am calm. I am emboldened by my own shining abilities.

I love my life and the ups and downs that have made me who I am today. I am a treasure chest full of experience and wisdom.

I drop the need to be perfect. I'm a creation machine. I just go, go, go.

I am bold and courageous. I always look for new ways to do things. If something unexpected happens, I celebrate the learning.

I am a powerhouse of love for myself, and I can do anything.

I feel my aliveness in each moment, in everything I do. I have raw power in my words, thoughts, actions, and movement.

I am passionate about my creativity, and I swim in a sea of inspiration.

I am unique, and so are my ideas. We are all unique.

I mine every fail for golden nuggets of wisdom. They're always there to be found.

I don't fear failure, because I love to experiment, and whatever happens, I just get smarter.

I pat myself on my own back. I show myself what I'm made of every day. I am rich with love and success.

I live the most brilliant life, one filled with shiny days and twinkly nights.

I am relaxed. Deep breath in, deep breath out. My body feels good. All is well.

My courage is strong, and it fuels my victories, no matter how many mountains I climb to get there.

I soar through failures like an eagle in the clouds. I wake up with a smile. I overflow with waterfalls of gratitude for life.

My best life is here. Full of lessons and learning. I am happy. So very, very happy.

Creativity Tip: Focus on Your Senses

We humans are sensing, feeling machines. And when we take advantage of this fact, a whole world opens up. When we cut off our senses, we suffer, often unknowingly. When we ignore them, we miss out.

It's possible to use your senses as a kind of therapy. At any time you desire, simply focusing on your senses can transport you into other states of mind.

Take a moment to focus on each of your senses individually, one by one. People have a tendency to focus on their sight, but setting aside ten minutes to pay close attention to your other senses is a great way to rev up your creativity.

For instance, try sitting down to dinner wearing a blindfold and with earplugs, and really focus on the taste of your food, and its texture in your mouth. Or roast some onions, and revel in the smell. Eat ice cream, and explore the sweet chill on your tongue. Run your fingertips over sandpaper, and thoroughly examine the grit. You'll be amazed at what you've been missing! When you take some time to give each of your senses some one-on-one, personal attention, you'll open a whole new world for creative exploration.

CHAPTER 18

WINE SELF-TALK SCRIPT: THE BOREDOM SECRET

Boredom always precedes a period of great creativity.

— Robert M. Pirsig

Imagine sitting in a room without your phone. There's no TV, no technology, no music, no book... no *nothing*... except for a comfortable chair and your thoughts. Does this scenario freak you out?

If you grew up in the age of smartphones, the thought of being stuck somewhere without your phone might make you uncomfortable. In a study from the University of Virginia, some students were actually willing to *shock* themselves—like, with *electricity*—rather than sit alone in their boredom with no phone. Um, crazy?

Do you feel the same way? If you accidentally dropped your phone into the toilet, and you didn't have a car to get to the store to buy a new one, and then the cable went out so you couldn't use your computer or watch TV... in other words, if you didn't have anything to do... would it make you a bit batty? Does the idea of sitting in your family room, or your kitchen nook, with nothing to do sound dreadful? (Note: I am *not* asking this question to new moms, haha! I remember those days when I would've given my left foot to zone out and stare at a wall.)

Well, the reason that boredom is generally regarded as an unpleasant emotion is because, when we're bored, we perceive time as ticking by at a painfully slow pace. Painful enough, in fact, that some of those University of Virginia students preferred to endure the physical pain of an electric shock.

I used to think I could never go to the gym or on a walk without my music or my cell phone. I would rather stay home working at my laptop than walk for 30 minutes with only my thoughts. How boring, right? I definitely understand why people want to avoid being bored.

But I feel very differently about boredom now. These days, I happily throw on my running shoes and head outside without my earbuds. Without my phone. Because I now realize how powerful "boring" time can be! Sounds crazy, I know... but stick with me... because with more boredom in your life, you can actually *increase your creativity*. And now I'm going to share a little secret...

The Boredom Secret

Most people don't know that boredom—that is, periods of non-stimulating, low mental activity—is actually really good for you. It's a specific kind of relaxation, and it's good for your brain. It doesn't mean you don't, at other times, relax with a book or a nap, but these serve different purposes. Intentionally taking time for boredom can have incredible benefits for your health and creativity.

In a fascinating TED Talk, *How Boredom Can Lead to Your Most Brilliant Ideas*, Manoush Zomorodi says,"When you get bored, you ignite a network in your brain called the default mode."

When this autopilot mode in your brain activates, it's a bit like spacing out, chilling, with an open, non-directed mind. And this is a very good thing when it comes to thinking outside the box. That is, outside the bounds of where your normal, more focused and task-oriented brain spends most of its time every day.

Strangely enough, despite feeling bored, your brain is actually *doing stuff* in this mode. During this time, your mind is wandering, and your brain *makes itself* busy—even though it might not feel like it—and this triggers creativity. It allows for mental exploration, imagination, and daydreaming. These are powerful capabilities of your brain, and this is when your brain makes most of its new and innovative connections. It can be where some of your *best ideas* come from!

Why does this happen when we're bored? Experts think that, because the situation or environment seems "lacking" (i.e., boring), the brain actively looks for new ways to overcome the boredom, and in doing so, it makes up new stuff to think about. How cool!

Why isn't this superpower more well-known? Why don't we all tap into it more often? Simply put, most of us are busy, most of the time. And when we're not busy, we're easily distracted, because our attention has value, and companies do almost anything to capture as much of it as possible. As a result, we live in a world where the swipe of your finger brings instant gratification in the form of entertainment or other diversions, such as news, scandal, gossip, and the like. I mean, we all like funny cat videos, right? And during the tiny breaks between all of those, we're bombarded by a constant flow of advertising.

But the problem is, in this technology-driven, media-packed world, you get very few moments for silence—lack of mental stimulation—unless you actively carve them out of your day, or turn off your devices. As a result, many of us never get to intimately know our minds.

And when you're constantly distracted, you also run the risk of high levels of stress and anxiety, because you don't take enough high-quality downtime. Sure, kicking back with a book or a good movie helps you rest and relieve some stress... but as I explained above, these aren't the same as taking some time to do nothing, letting your mind wander, and seeing what it comes up with all by itself.

> *Solitude is creativity's best friend, and solitude is refreshment for our souls.*
>
> — NAOMI JUDD

So take advantage of boredom, and loosen the stranglehold on your creativity by spending a little time with no mental stimulation. The next time you have a few minutes with nothing to do, don't reach for your phone. Don't look for a task to make you feel productive. Instead, just sit or stand there, and let your mind go blank. Or wander. And if you don't have 15 minutes to do nothing, then maybe it's time to schedule that into your day. It's what I did before I was able to make it a habit. I made a *date with boredom*.

Make a Date with Boredom

When I learned that boredom can be an incredible source of creativity, my ears perked up. I mean, I'm all about finding ways to increase my creativity. Creativity reduces anxiety, it's fun, it supercharges your career, and well, frankly, it's one of the best-kept secrets of longevity: Creative people live longer.

That said, the idea made me a little nervous. I mean... boredom? Isn't that wasting time, virtually by definition? You know, doing nothing? That didn't sit too well with my aggressive, go-go personality. I eyed the research with a bit of skepticism. But what the neuroscientists were saying made sense: If I don't do anything with my brain (including consuming *other people's* creative output, like books, TV, movies, or even music), then my brain will kinda be forced to do something *on its own*. Ok, that made sense... that was something I could at least accept on faith, enough to experiment with.

So I gave it a try.

Honestly, it took me a while to get comfortable with "doing nothing." I kept wondering if I should sneak in little blips of productive thinking—like thinking about my to-do list while I'm doing nothing—and then I'd catch myself. *Stop it, Kristen! That defeats the whole purpose!*

It was also difficult to break the physical habit of reaching for my phone during all those little pauses during the day. I'd reach for it without even thinking, and then catch myself, and set the phone back down.

But after the first few times of really experiencing doing nothing... boredom... I've gotta say, I felt *so much better.* I became much more relaxed, not always being "on," which is how I feel when my eyes are glued to my phone.

Then, in short order, the stuff the scientists talked about actually started to happen to me! Ideas started to swirl around my head. *New thoughts! New ideas!*

I became a raving fan. Yeah, being bored is cool.

So give this a try yourself. Make a habit in which you don't bring your phone with you. Such as when going for walks, or when you take the dogs outside. Or while waiting in line at the grocery store, simply leave your phone in your purse, and stare off into space. Or the next time you're driving to work, don't listen to the radio, don't put on any podcasts. Just drive along with the hum of the engine as your only company. Sure, it's an adjustment at first. But like everything else we do, the more times you allow yourself the pleasure of doing nothing, the easier it gets.

And from there, wait and see what happens. Don't be surprised if boredom becomes your new BFF, and if you start having richer, more interesting and creative thoughts, more and more often.

On her popular blog, *The Marginalian* (formerly *Brain Pickings*) Maria Popova writes,

> *Build pockets of stillness into your life. Meditate. Go for walks. Ride your bike going nowhere in particular. There is a creative purpose to daydreaming, even to boredom. The best ideas come to us when we stop actively trying to coax the muse into manifesting and let the fragments of experience float around our unconscious mind in order to click into new combinations.*

~

The following script will help you comfortably, and without guilt, explore the space that boredom creates for your brain to unfold its wings and tap into your inner genius.

Wine Self-Talk Script: The Boredom Secret

I love when my mind wanders. It feels so relaxing.

I give my mind time to run free, with no restrictions, no barriers or precursors. Be free, mind! Be free!

Daydreaming is a powerful way to increase my creativity. It helps my brain make more connections and come up with new ideas.

When I'm bored, I solve problems and find answers to questions. It's a superpower of mine.

My mind happily wanders through the space of emptiness. No end goal, no end result, just wandering, relaxing, and exploring.

I am relaxed. I am calm. I am living my best life.

I'm in the right place at the right time.

My life is a creative fairytale land of adventure and promise. I take it all step-by-step, easy breezy, and I have an abundance of time to do everything I want to do.

My self-love boosts my creativity. Taking time for my mind to play is rewarding.

I am worthy of taking time for boredom. To chill out, with no phone or distractions. Run, beautiful mind, run, and have fun!

I love being bored. It stimulates all kinds of new ideas, clever solutions, and unique connections.

When I give my mind and body the space and freedom to explore, to tinker on its own, I'm happy.

Boredom feels like silky caresses to my mind. I'm relaxed, and I love this special, free time with my mind.

I am touched at my own quiet power that rises through me. I am worthy. So very, very worthy.

I let my mind run. I take it on playdates full of wandering, stardust, and outer space. My life is amazing.

Taking time for boredom is an act of self-care. My love for myself shimmers beneath my skin. This is MY time.

I glide through my day, it's effortless, I feel like I float on clouds of love.

I look forward to giving my mind time to unwind.

Boredom is easy. It feels right. I welcome it into my day. I engineer the most incredible ideas when I simply take the time to do nothing.

Creativity Tip: Do Something Else

When working on a project, taking breaks gives you a chance to refresh your mind and recharge. This way, when you come back to the project, you have increased creativity and energy.

One of my favorite ways to do this happens when I'm working on a book. At the end of a scene or a chapter, I'll get up and step away from my desk to do something else. Even if I know exactly what I'm going to write next, I still get up and do something else.

Artists and experts have been doing this for millennia, knowing that brief breaks often breed creativity. So, if I have phone calls to make that day, I'll stop writing, mid-chapter, to make one of the calls. Or I'll go to the bathroom, or let the dogs out, or get something to eat, or make another cup of coffee.

The point is to *interrupt* the work. Take a break, and come back to it refreshed. It works every time.

CHAPTER 19

WINE SELF-TALK SCRIPT: THE HUMOR-CREATIVITY CONNECTION

> *What's the difference between a poorly dressed man on a unicycle and a well-dressed man on a bicycle? Attire.*
>
> — READER'S DIGEST JOKES

Laughing is great for many things, but did you know that there's a connection between humor and creativity? As it happens, when we have more humor in our lives, we do more creative thinking. According to Psychology.com,

> *Research shows that people in a lighter mood experience more eureka moments and greater inspiration.*

Boy oh boy, this is so super true for me. When I really get going, laughing my ass off, I start spewing all kinds of wacky stuff, which is good! That means creativity is happening!

Laughter: A Powerful Experience

We laugh for different reasons. Humor is often related to some kind of mistake... think banana peel pratfalls and hilarious misunderstandings in sitcoms. Which is one of the main reasons humor can be beneficial to your creativity. When you can laugh at a mistake, it makes you more confident and open to taking chances. With this mindset, you don't fear making mistakes, and this allows you to be more creative because you're willing to experiment, looking for connections between far-flung ideas.

Too often, we shy away from taking risks, not for fear of harm, but fear of embarrassment. If you can cultivate the attitude of "oh well" and shrug things off, you'll be more lighthearted in your endeavors, and better off.

When I make a mistake, one of the things I routinely say to keep myself motivated and uplifted is the famous line, *Someday, I'll laugh about this.*

And isn't that so often true? Isn't it interesting that something we perceive as bad in the moment can make for a funny story in the future? Why is that?

Perspective. Which is what we gain with the passage of time.

Why not remind yourself of that in the present? There's no need to wait for the future to exercise wisdom.

So remind yourself of that the next time you make a mistake or have a fabulous fail. In this way, humor keeps encouraging creative risk-taking. It gives you permission to be goofy and whimsical. Many of the best ideas seem a little crazy, remember? If something were obvious, everybody would already be doing it.

Running toward the goofy, whimsical, and crazy breaks down the barriers—like convention and old habits—to free your mind to take a new approach, or to get started on some new creative project. If you feel free to make mistakes, you're more likely to just jump in and start working on something. Which is always better than doing nothing.

> *My mother wanted us to understand that the tragedies of your life one day have the potential to be comic stories the next.*
>
> — *Nora Ephron*

Another kind of humor is called *comic relief*... which is humor that relieves tension when suspense or dread is overwhelming. This kind of humor is a great tool if you find yourself depressed, losing heart, or in a rut, thinking about the same things over and over. Or if you feel tight with anxiety. Taking time to simply read jokes or watch something funny online, maybe something about cats and cucumbers (Google it... haha), it can snap you right out of that mental loop. Humor is perfect for creating more *mental space*, clearing out the yellow police tape in your head, and making it easier to come up with solutions or make novel connections.

And, as you might imagine, when you have humor in your life, you're more relaxed. And the increase in relaxation will help your brain make better connections. In other words, increase creativity. It's much easier to do great work when you're less stressed.

In a study from Northwestern University, researchers studied two groups of participants. One group watched a comedy movie, and another group watched a horror movie. After the movies, both groups were given a word association puzzle to solve. And guess what... the group that watched the comedy was more creative at solving the puzzle!

Neuroscientists have discovered through EEG brain scans that humor and laughter are complex cognitive functions that light up the entire brain, both the left side and the right side. They each play a role when processing humor.

Think of your brain like a Christmas tree, with twinkling lights running all through it. Those blinking lights are like laughter, which is produced from a circuit that runs through many regions of your brain (the Christmas tree). This is how experts believe humor helps enhance learning and creativity—by stimulating many areas in both sides of the brain simultaneously. In this sense, "connections" aren't just metaphorical; they're literally connections between different parts of your brain that harbor different thought patterns and knowledge.

Humor also develops your *divergent thinking skills*, which is when your brain zigs and zags, as opposed to thinking in a more straightforward, conventional way. Divergent thinking is central to many types of humor, and it does wonders for creativity. It's the source of something called *exaptation*, which means using things for something other than their intended purpose. It happens in nature, such as when dinosaurs had early versions of feathers for warmth, and then some of the dinosaurs *exapted* these feathers into wings, ultimately leading to the flight in birds we see today.

Many modern companies come up with their genius inventions by merely exapting older technologies and using them in new ways. For instance, sending digital data over telephone lines that were designed to carry people's voices. Or the engineers who tinkered with an inkjet printer, hacking it to squirt out melted plastic instead of ink, and inventing the entire new industry of 3D printing!

This kind of hacking ability is highly sought in the world's most innovative companies. In fact, a standard type of job interview question at many such companies involves handing the candidate some ordinary object, such as a pen, and asking her to name ten things she could do with the pen, other than writing. And wouldn't you know it... a lot of the answers end up being *funny*. Because the best answers will often be absurd, clever, and wacky. And guess what? That's the candidate they hire!

More Laughter = *More Abundance*

Laughter is energizing, which plays a large role in creativity. When I laugh, I am energized, and this puts me in a great mindset for smashing through my goals and manifesting my dreams. In my mind, I've linked laughter with more success and abundance, and that perspective isn't uncommon. According to *Psychology Today*, when a study by the McClelland Centre for Research and Innovation looked at executive compensation, they found a direct correlation between the use of humor and the size of the executives' compensation. The funnier they were, the more money they made!

If you're an executive, team leader, or a business owner, then encouraging laughter can be a great team-building exercise and help improve your company's culture by creating a fun atmosphere. This is because genuine laughter usually exists between people who trust each other, and building trust boosts productivity and employee satisfaction.

Get in a Good Mood!

It turns out that sadness inhibits the creation of new ideas. Um, not surprising. When you're sad, you're less able to see opportunities and potential. And even if you can see them, you're less likely to feel motivated or take action.

But, good news, the opposite is also true! Those researchers at Northwestern found that creative insight was correlated with boosted activity in a part of the brain called the *anterior cingulate cortex* (ACC). People in happy moods displayed boosted ACC activity on a functional MRI before solving a set of problems, which the researchers believe helped the subjects find solutions to the problems.

In other studies supporting this finding, when people are happy, it's easier for them to come up with unique word associations, story ideas, and they're better at solving moral dilemmas. All because you're in a good mood!

Fortunately, there's a fantastic way to whip your mood into heavenly happiness... *self-talk!*

Happiness even helps doctors. In Shawn Achor's book, *The Happiness Advantage*, he describes how doctors who were put in a good mood before making diagnoses showed almost *three times* better diagnostic ability and creativity than doctors in a neutral state. And the speed of the accurate diagnoses increased. I mean... *WTF?* Well, it turns out that our brains are wired to perform best when we're happy, and not when they're negative, or even neutral. (Pro-tip: The next time you're headed into surgery, *make sure your doc is in a good mood!)*

Add Some Humor into Your Life

If you're not laughing quite a bit, every day, take a look at your environment and your leisure activities. Are there any areas you can improve?

You might start watching more comedies, subscribe to joke-a-day email newsletters, watch hilarious YouTube videos, take an improv class, or spend more time around any funny people you know. (And if you're dating, be sure to put *sense of humor* high on your list of requirements! There's perhaps no better way to spend your days and years than with a partner who makes you laugh!)

If you've read *Coffee Self-Talk*, you know that I've minimized a lot of my daily exposure to social media, in a deliberate strategy to shield my brain and my magical life from pointless toxicity. That said, I do make a point to follow *super funny folks* on Twitter. Just ask my husband... when he hears me start howling with laughter, and sees me *literally crying* because I'm laughing so hard, it's 100% always because of something that came across my Twitter feed!

~

The following script will help you foster more humor in your life, to help tap into your inner creative genius.

Wine Self-Talk Script: The Humor-Creativity Connection

I love being funny! I have a knack for seeing the humor in life.

Laughing is one of my favorite ways to relax.

I love humor, and humor loves me.

If I make a mistake, I laugh it off like the funny thing it is. This keeps my feelings elevated, and that keeps me zooming along on the creativity train.

The more I laugh at things, the easier it is to laugh even more.

By honing my humor skills, I'm training my brain to go in unexpected directions, which helps me live a magical, creative life.

I have incredibly fresh ideas when I'm happy and laughing.

My positivity is contagious. By making others around me laugh, we all trust each other more.

Bustin' a gut from a case of the chuckles lights me up with smiles.

Giggle! Tee hee! Haha! Hehe!

Humor can be found everywhere. We are all worthy of a life full of laughs.

I love imagining myself having huge belly laughs, full of snorts and guffaws. Laughter really does make the world go round.

The more I laugh, giggle, and chuckle, the more creative I am.

I surround myself with funny, loving people, and we have a grand time. Everyone deserves smiles, laughter, and love.

Being able to make jokes is my specialty. Using props in the wrong way leads to humor and inspiration. Puns are perfect to add light-hearted fun to language, thinking in new and novel ways.

I meet funny people all the time. So many, that sometimes I spend my whole day laughing.

I laugh, and laugh, and laugh, and then I laugh some more. Hahahaha!

I roar and shake with laughter, silly and playful. This lightens the mood in the room, and it creates space in my mind. I am a creative genius.

Looking at things from different angles, using both the left and right sides of my brain, keeps me distinctive, fresh, and innovative.

I have eureka moments! They blaze through my mind. I am constantly inspired to be my best and live my best life.

When I'm laughing, I know my brain is lighting up all over, like shooting stars in the night sky. Making connections. Novelty being born. I feel so alive! Zoom! Bam! Shazam!

Creativity Tip: Mission Help Others

Ryan Holiday, author of *Ego Is the Enemy*, writes about something he calls the *Canvas Strategy*, where you "create a canvas" upon which other people can create (metaphorical) art. By providing them with this creative space, you make others look good, and meanwhile, you gain knowledge, expertise, and influence. When I first read about it, it struck me as a great tip for increasing creativity. Holiday writes,

> *Imagine if, for every person you met, you thought of some way to help them, something you could do for them? And you looked at it in a way that entirely benefited them and not you? The cumulative effect this would have over time would be profound: You'd learn a great deal by solving diverse problems. You'd develop a reputation for being indispensable. You'd have countless new relationships.*

This is a brilliant way to make new connections in your mind and spark creativity. It's an experience that provides you with ample material to strengthen your problem-solving muscle, to stretch your *new ideas* muscle, and to feel good the whole time because you'll be helping others.

CHAPTER 20

CHAMPAGNE SELF-TALK: CELEBRATING YOUR GOLDEN CREATIVITY

> *One must still have chaos in oneself to be able to give birth to a dancing star.*
>
> — Friedrich Nietzsche

It's time to celebrate!

Yay! You're on the last lesson for tapping into your inner genius with Wine Self-Talk. Congratulations! That is definitely cause for celebration.

Today, we're going to do something very fun: replace the wine you sip during your ritual with Champagne!

Why?

Because 1) Champagne is fun, and 2) it's the perfect way to magnify the emotional feeling of *celebration*.

The Importance of Celebrating

Why is celebrating important? Because it focuses your mind and heart on something specific about the moment. It produces a bit of sparkling magic, simply by drawing your attention to something that might have otherwise gone unnoticed, and saying, *Hey, this is important enough to celebrate.*

When you celebrate a thing, you make it special. In this way, you can transform anything into something special.

Celebrations can be big, like a party, or rewarding yourself with a fancy vacation or a weekend getaway. Celebrations can be medium-sized, like taking the afternoon off, or going shopping. Or they can be tiny but notable *micro-celebrations*, such as having a glass of wine (or Champagne!), or making a toast, or simply thinking to yourself in a private moment, *Congratulations. Well done.*

Which brings me to my first point: In every aspect of your life, start celebrating everything, big and small. Celebrate when you finish a chapter in a book. And then celebrate when you finish the whole book. Celebrate when you get to the gym during a busy day. Celebrate when you get a good night's sleep. Celebrate taking time for your self-talk.

Celebrate it all!

Maybe I should have put this chapter at the beginning, haha... so you'd celebrate every chapter along the way!

Celebrating is a special form of gratitude. It's very powerful, and it's an underused tool in the success toolkit that we all have available to us, at all times. Celebration does not lose its juice, even when you celebrate almost everything. If anything, it does the exact opposite... it builds momentum and keeps the exciting, high-vibrational energy flowing through your day. More high-fives. More smiles. And more *reasons* to celebrate, because you start to notice them more.

And what does this mean for you?

More fun. Less anxiety. More creativity. More manifesting. More magic.

Celebrating can be very simple. It doesn't require spending money or eating some kind of treat. At least, not every time. But feel free to splurge for the *BIG* stuff! Oh, and despite the instructions for this script, celebrating certainly doesn't have to be accompanied with Champagne... although, I think we'd all agree, it's fun from time to time!

Celebrating can mean simply dancing around the house. It can be done with high-fives. Or big, gigantic hugs. Celebrating can be done with taking time off and giving yourself an extra break to do something fun or relaxing. Celebrating comes in all different fashions, and life is much more magical when you celebrate just about everything you do.

Life is for celebrating. It's meant to be lived *big*. You are meant to live huge, arms open wide, smiles so big they split your face in half. That's epic living. Legendary. *Magical.*

So, let's get more of that magic into our lives by deciding, right now, to celebrate *more things, more often*. Take a moment, and think about the things you do on any given week. Cooking a meal? Calling a friend? Exercising? Making progress toward... anything? And when you accomplish those things, assign some type of celebration to each one. Get into the habit of celebrating everything. Even when things don't go as planned, there is always a silver lining to be found, and so celebrate *that*, too.

Visioneering the Celebration of Your Creative Success

I have another exciting way that I use the act of celebrating: for manifesting and making my dreams come true.

Visioneering is a term I use to describe "engineering my visions of my future," which, among other things, includes visualization with a strong emotional component. In other words, when you visualize, you want to feel feelings, not just see pictures.

When I visioneer my future successes regarding creativity, I close my eyes, and I often visualize other people celebrating my success with me, to heighten the emotional resonance. I imagine friends or family sitting across from me at the dinner table, congratulating me, toasting me with glasses of Champagne because I've accomplished something creative, such as inventing something, or writing a new book.

I imagine how I would feel celebrating my creative endeavors. I see it in my mind. I feel the good feelings that would be there. I taste the pink Champagne, imagining the bubbles effervescing on my tongue. In my mind, I hear what people would be saying to me... *"Congratulations, Kristen! You did it!"* High-fives all around, and joyful laughter throughout the room envisioned in my mind.

I love doing this as I drift off to sleep at night, too. Or before a nap. I make a story in my mind, picturing the scene, and I get very specific about the details: the room, the decor, the people, the chairs we're sitting in. One of my go-to scenes is to imagine my mom sitting across from me on her beige loveseat, and she's congratulating me on some accomplishment related to whatever goal I'm working on.

I play out the whole scene in my mind. She's sitting there, with her high, blonde ponytail, leopard scarf tied around it. Her makeup is flawless. *"Kristen!" she beams. "Congratulations! My god, you did it. I'm so happy for you!"* We hug a big, long, tight hug. Then, a huge sloppy grin spreads across my face, and I say back to her, *"Yes! Thank you! I did it!"* And I victoriously punch my fist into the air. (I actually do the punch; I don't just visualize it.)

The first time I did this little exercise, we were living in our tiny apartment in Italy, buried under a mountain of debt. I visualized what my life would be like after experiencing a financial success and paying off the debt. In particular, I focused on how I would *feel* in such a situation. I didn't think about the financial details, or even the nature of the success. This is important... because I didn't yet have an actual plan, I didn't know exactly how we'd ever see our financial success, but *I believed it would happen*. I *experienced* it emotionally. And it felt so real!

So, in spite of my circumstances, I was giddy with excitement for all of the opportunities that I believed would fall into our lap, one way or another. And on many nights, I would fall asleep imagining the scenario of my mom and me celebrating my success.

The first couple of times I did it, it was a little weird. I felt as though I was witnessing the scene play out from a distance, like an out-of-body experience, or watching it as a movie on a screen. But after a few times, it really started to viscerally feel real, and that was the key. It elevated my emotions, making me a true believer. It caused me to genuinely *expect* this vision of the future to come true.

Just over a year later, it did come true. Almost that exact scene! Though Mom wasn't wearing her leopard scarf, and we were sitting in different chairs. We were visiting my mom in Arizona, and she was congratulating me on the success of *Coffee Self-Talk*, which had become a bestseller. As she sat there congratulating me—in real life—the scene was uncanny in its similarity to my visualization. It felt like *déjà vu*.

With visualization, picturing the details is important. As many details as possible. And, in particular, feeling the emotions. This will get your heart and mind in sync, so they're pulling in the same direction.

Especially when you don't yet actually know which path to follow—when you don't yet have a plan, or you haven't yet decided on a course of action—then don't worry about the tactical details. Just focus on the emotions.

Go ahead and try it yourself. Imagine people congratulating you on your success, even if you don't know right now what they're congratulating you about. Try to feel the energy in the room... the joy, the warmth, the love and admiration. And be sure to imagine the sound of clinking glasses!

Champagne Self-Talk, Anyone?

And, of course, if you typically drink wine when you do your Wine Self-Talk, then consider switching to some bubbly when you do celebratory Wine Self-Talk. (You can also just add some sparkling water to your wine.) Champagne, Prosecco, sparkling apple cider, or even sparkling water—any of these can add effervescence, lightness, and airy celebration to the ritual, immediately shifting your mindset into Celebration Mode, and laying the groundwork for many future celebrations to come.

Champagne Self-Talk Script: Celebrating Your Golden Creativity

I am radically happy. I jump for joy. Why? Because I can. Yes, because I can. RAAAHHHHH! I'm popping like a cork off a bottle of pink Champagne. Pow!

Champagne! I toast to myself. I toast to my life. I toast to my accomplishments. The bubbles in my mouth, dancing on my tongue, cheering me on.

I feel the fire, burning in my bones, lighting me up. I'm completely abloom. Brighter, brighter, brighter! Here I go!

My spirit soars, my power is ready to burst out of me. I'm standing proud to the world. I celebrate me!

I open my arms. I hug myself. I smile. I relax. I celebrate my life.

Iridescence, illumination, shimmer shine. That's the energy I radiate from my rock-solid foundation of love and worthiness. I am beautiful. I celebrate me.

My life is a bright, glimmering gem, because I make it so. I choose to be happy with it all, a shooting star. I feel so amazing, so alive! YEAHH!

I give myself a toast, my blood sparkles like it's filled with bubbly Champagne. Lifting me up and up and up.

I am victorious. I see it now. I feel it in my bones. It's a part of me, celebrating.

I'm walking through my new life, celebrating it all, through glittering diamond doors of love and opportunity, fresh, bright, and sparkling.

I'm a winner. I'm standing on top of my life, on top of my world, like a champion. I'm going for it, going for the gold, my heart, loving me forever.

Confetti, glitter, and Champagne popping all around. I wake up every morning imagining all the wonderful things to celebrate.

I love celebrating. Celebrating loves me!

I adore my life.

I am worthy of living a life full of celebrations. We all are.

I experience pleasure today. Oodles and oodles of silky pleasure.

The colors of my skies are infinite, and they light me up, sparkling high, high, high. I am amazing. I am love.

Thank you, life. Thank you, me. For taking time to celebrate.

It's a great day for living my best life. It's always a great day for celebrating. Starting here. Starting now.

My mindset is primed for celebration, and I am primed for success.

Creativity Tip: Take on a New Challenge

Make a list of ways you can challenge your creativity by doing things that you haven't done before. Or things that you haven't done in a while. For example, getting out a crazy-hard jigsaw puzzle and setting it up on your dining room table. Or getting out a coloring book and magic markers, and plopping them down on the kitchen table. (I love coloring. It brings out the kid in me.)

Or it can be doing something completely new, like getting together with a group of friends and visiting an *escape room* for a wild adventure that lights up your creativity circuits. That's the whole purpose of it! Or going to one of those "blackout" dining restaurants, where you're blindfolded, eating a multi-course menu in total darkness. Or taking dance classes. Or trying a new sport, like tennis, or pickle ball, or golf!

Or it could be calling up friends and family and saying, *Do you have any challenges right now? Because I'd like to exercise my creativity and try to help you come up with solutions.*

It doesn't matter what you choose. Any of these will be great for increasing your relaxation, decreasing anxiety, and throwing gasoline on your creativity fires. *Light yourself up, baby!*

CONCLUSION & FREE GOODIES

So there you have it! *Wine Self-Talk.*

I'm excited for you and your new journey with wildly brilliant creativity. I'm eager to see where this new ritual takes you!

As I wrote about in Part I, when you have creativity in your life as a partner, it helps with everything. It makes life more fun, more magical. So strike out, and go forth boldly in the direction of whatever creative passion is calling you. See more magic and color in your life. Create something from your heart. Relax your mind under the stars. Give yourself permission to imagine the infinite opportunities of your potential. And take your rests! Schedule them, and suck the juice from life by giving yourself some leisure time. *You deserve it!*

And finally, celebrate all of your wins, big and small. Celebrate them even before they happen, and in doing so, *make them happen*. Celebrate your creativity. Celebrate your ideas. Go big! We're all waiting for you to explode onto the scene with glittering success and fireworks. I'm excited to see what you create. What problems you solve. What new options you create for yourself. And how much *more magical* your life is as a result.

Free Goodies!

Shoot me an email to receive a free PDF with:

- Printable versions of the scripts in this book
- *Creativity Starter Questions* for your Wine Self-Talk ritual
- Bonus Chapter: *Star Time to Open Your Mind*

Email me at:

Kristen@KristenHelmstetter.com

Please specify that you'd like the "*Wine Self-Talk goodies.*"

~

I have a HUGE favor to ask of you.

If you would help me, I'd greatly appreciate it. I'd love it if you would leave a review for this book on Amazon. Reviews are incredibly important for authors, and I'm extremely grateful if you would write one!

~

I'd love to hear from you and your experiences when you add Wine Self-Talk to your life!

Email me at:

Kristen@KristenHelmstetter.com

Or find me at:

Instagram.com/coffeeselftalk

You can hear me every week on the *Coffee Self-Talk with Kristen Helmstetter* podcast here, or wherever you listen to podcasts:

https://anchor.fm/kristen-helmstetter

And come join our fun and lively group for readers:

Facebook.com/groups/coffeeselftalk

I'm so looking forward to hearing from you!

~

What's Next?

Here are the other books in the Coffee Self-Talk family:

International Bestseller – Over 100,000 Copies Sold

Coffee Self-Talk: 5 Minutes a Day to Start Living Your Magical Life

Coffee Self-Talk is a powerful, life-changing routine that takes only 5 minutes a day. What if you could wake up every morning feeling more incredible than ever before... in 5 minutes? **Living the most epic life. Your mind mastered!** Coffee Self-Talk transforms your life by boosting your self-esteem, filling you with happiness, and helping you attract the magical life you dream of living. ***All this, with your next cup of coffee.***

The Coffee Self-Talk Daily Reader #1:

Bite-Sized Nuggets of Magic to Add to Your Morning Ritual

This companion book offers short, daily reads for tips and inspiration. It does not replace your daily Coffee Self-Talk routine. Rather, it's meant to be used each day *after* you do your Coffee Self-Talk.

If you do one reading per day, it will take 30 days to complete.

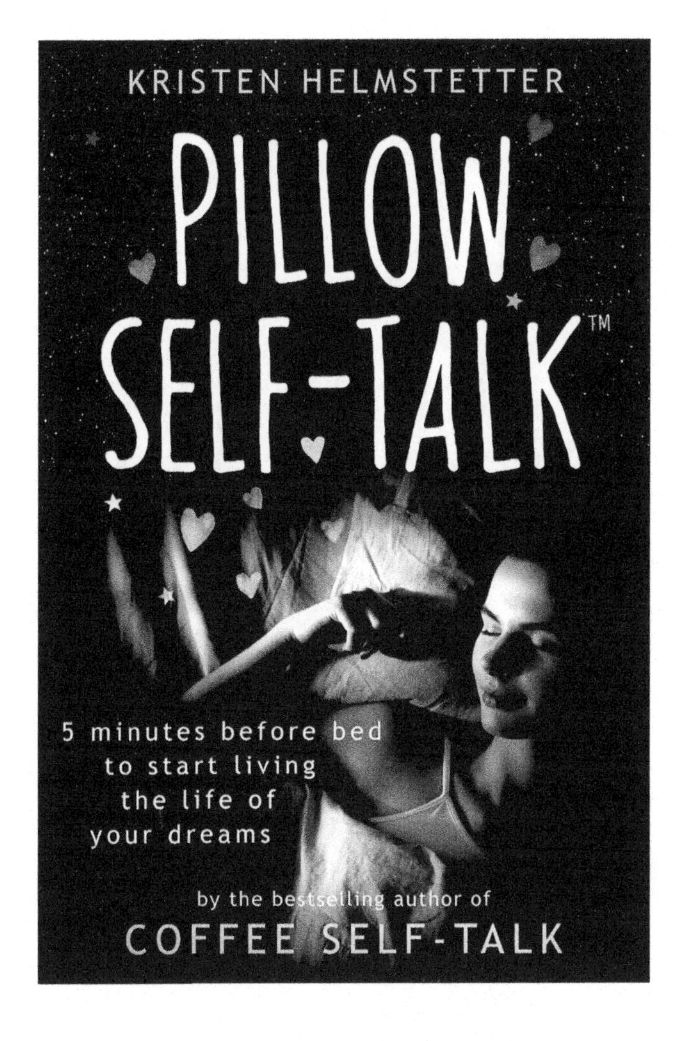

Pillow Self-Talk: 5 Minutes Before Bed to Start Living the Life of Your Dreams

End your day with a powerful nighttime ritual to help you manifest your dreams, reach your goals, find peace, relaxation, and happiness... all while getting the *best sleep ever!*

KRISTEN HELMSTETTER

COFFEE SELF-TALK™

GUIDED JOURNAL

Writing Prompts & Inspiration for Living Your Magical Life

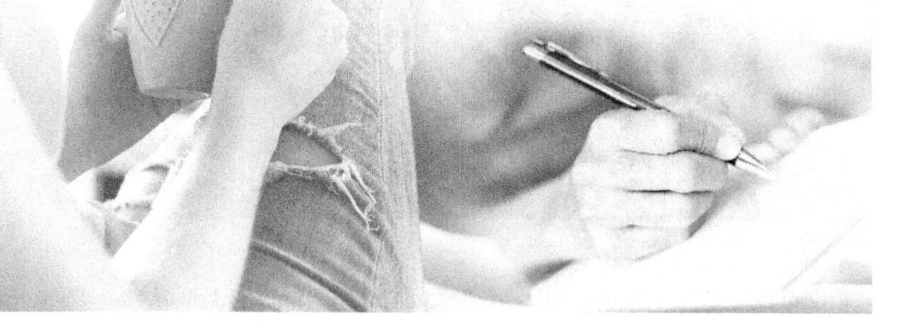

The Coffee Self-Talk Guided Journal:

Writing Prompts & Inspiration for Living Your Magical Life

This guided journal keeps you *lit up and glowing* as you go deeper into your magical Coffee Self-Talk journey. Experience the joy of journaling, mixed with fun, thought-provoking exercises, and discover hidden gems about yourself. Get inspired, slash your anxiety, and unleash your amazing, badass self.

The Coffee Self-Talk Blank Journal

This is literally a blank journal (with lines). There are no words, except for a one-page intro.

This blank journal provides a place to write your own scripts, as well as journal your thoughts and progress. You could use any notebook, but readers have asked for a matching journal to make things fun and help reinforce their daily Coffee Self-Talk ritual.

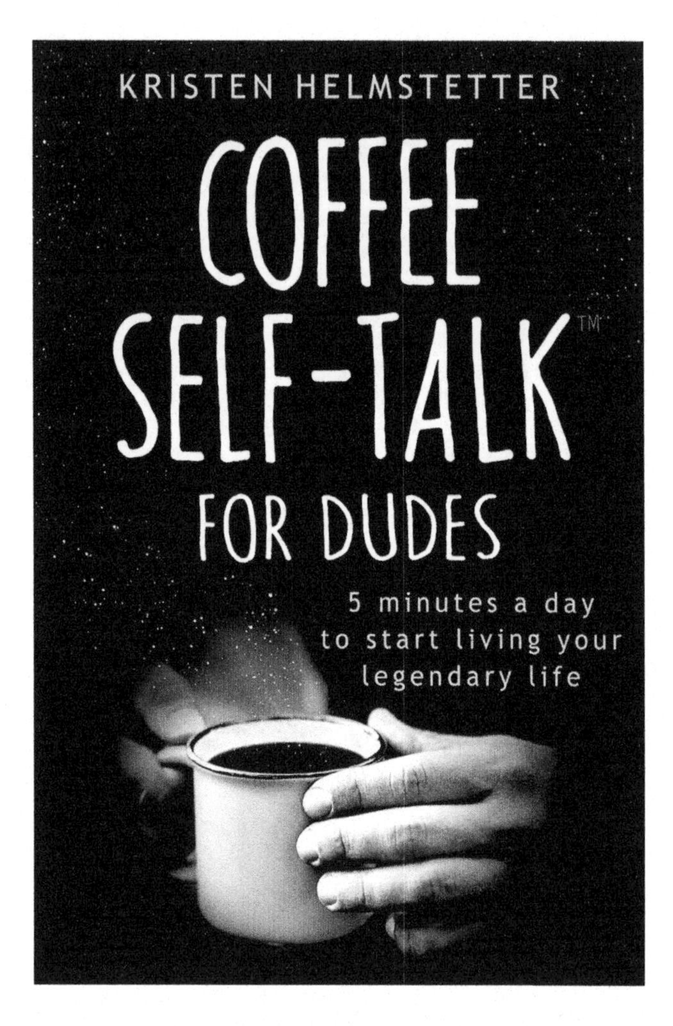

Coffee Self-Talk for Dudes:

5 Minutes a Day to Start Living Your Legendary Life

This is a special edition of *Coffee Self-Talk* that has been edited to be more oriented toward men in the language, examples, and scripts. It is 95% identical to the original *Coffee Self-Talk* book.

Coffee Self-Talk for Teen Girls:

5 Minutes a Day for Confidence, Achievement & Lifelong Happiness

This is written for girls in high school (ages 13 to 17 years old). It covers the same ideas as *Coffee Self-Talk*, and applies them to the issues that teen girls face, such as school, grades, sports, peer pressure, social media, social anxiety, beauty/body issues, and dating.

Coffee Mugs & More

Visit CoffeeSelfTalk.com for all kinds of fun stuff to add more self-talk to your day:

- Coffee mugs
- Travel mugs
- Water bottles
- Notebooks
- And more

Readers of this book get a 10% discount (one-time use only). Just enter the following at checkout.

Coupon code: **CSTBOOK10%**

Made in United States
North Haven, CT
28 July 2022